A TWELVE OF HEARTS AND THE WARRIOR PRINCESS

By Ruth Edwards

Cover Design by Melinda E. Self

ISBN: 978-0-578-40087-7

Preface

I told a friend a few years ago that she would readily recognize me in heaven. I would be the one with my hand raised, asking all the questions. I think that will be okay with God and He will answer every one. Maybe there will be group sessions of us who want answers or even lecture halls full. OR as my husband has reminded me, "The questions won't matter then. It will all be clear the minute we get there."

I've asked plenty of questions here, too, variously answered and sometimes not.

Was our Teresa an ordinary girl who wanted to live an extraordinary life? Or was she an extraordinary girl who just wanted an ordinary life? If you had asked her in her late childhood, even before her diagnosis, and certainly in any of the years after that, I think she would have said that she just wanted to be a normal, ordinary person with a nice normal, ordinary life. What she turned out to have was indeed extraordinary, but she reached for the normal every minute of each day.

Was she given this mission of suffering as a gift to others, as someone once suggested? I don't know. What I do know is that her life intersected with the lives of countless people, ours and those who came our way, and God used that to urge so many into that larger self of love, compassion, helpfulness, prayerfulness, and dependence on Him.

Was her life a source of joy to those God gave her to love? Without a doubt.

Was the journey difficult? No affirmative response I can think of can answer this one strongly enough. We ran from the darkness so often and when it caught us we wrestled away as best we could with the help of God's children. One old spiritual that I remember so well sings about all God's children having a robe, wings, a harp, and shoes. Can we add light to that too? If we don't always have it with us, we know where to find it.

Why am I writing this book? And why now? Or why not until now? I started long ago. I have had many nudges from the angels, both heavenly and earthly. I especially think of my friends Peggy Cain and Edna Cook as I write that. Peggy kept my girls in her home when they were little and keeps them in her heart always. Peggy never stopped encouraging me to write Teresa's story. And my dear friend Edna would say, "Write the book, Ruth. I'm getting old and I want to read it." Edna, you will never seem old to me, just sweet and kind and wise and full of love for everyone. I wanted to sort it all out but have decided that waiting for it all to make sense could take a very long time, too long, maybe never. Too many stalled plans in too many yesterdays make for a lack of meaning in today and a dearth of clarity for tomorrow.

There is a fourteen-year-old boy and the man he will someday be who needs for me to write. He is Teresa's boy and one of the main reasons she fought and struggled so hard to stay here.

I pray you will feel our thankfulness throughout Teresa's memoir. God has been good. He has traveled with us. He taught us so much and continues to do that. He sent the earth angels who marched across Teresa's history. I hope many of them will see themselves in this story and maybe recognize what their acts of love did for Teresa and for her family. I can never include them all by name, but those mentioned are representative of the mass of good, good people who came to our rescue in every leg of the journey.

And maybe someone out there with a "twelve of hearts" needs to know that once there was a girl who was dealt a hand that none of us ever imagined would be hers, but who, with God's help, played it courageously and stared down her own mortality time and again, who never lost her belief in miracles, and who held tight to hope throughout a good, hard fight. I want you to know her.

It is important that every reader of this story understand that none of the characters who lived this is a saint. We were/are just ordinary people putting one foot in front of the other each day. We failed regularly. We got discouraged. Sometimes we felt a bit of injustice. We let fear, worry, doubt, and pity in sometimes when we shouldn't have. We probably didn't say "thank you" as often as we should have. We are still learning from the lessons taught throughout these many years. And we still believe that God had, has, and always will have a plan for each of us.

This story is told from my perspective, which is from a mother's heart. I have included some of Teresa's written and spoken words that may give you glimpses of how she felt at times along the way. But as close as I was to my daughter, as much as I suffered along with her, I cannot write from her perspective because I was never in the place that she was. Certainly I hope my perspective gives insight into **who** she was. I have wept for my husband's pain, for Teresa's husband's pain, for their son's pain, her sister's and other family members' sorrow, because, loving them, it was impossible not to feel it. But their perspective was not mine either. Almost everything I say in these pages, then, although it is Teresa's story, is through my eyes and heart, what I understood and didn't, and it is my processing of events.

Part One of Teresa's story I began writing in 1998. She was twenty-three years old as I starting pouring my heart out into my little word processor and it is a look back at her childhood, her diagnosis, and her life for nearly twelve years after that diagnosis. Part Two is a description of what I call "The Miracle Years," that amazing journey toward and through the transplant process. Part Three I've named "The Glory Years," Part Four the "Mystery Years," and the final section is about that last valiant fight in her journey and was probably the most difficult section to wring from my heart into text.

We realize that others, too, have suffered terrible tragedy in their lives. Every day that we listen to the TV news or read our newsfeeds, participate in social media, or interact within our own families, circles of friends and acquaintances, churches, workplaces, and communities, we can find someone sick, injured, wronged, or troubled. Physical, emotional, spiritual, mental, financial, social, and other ills... suffering. It is easy to think we have it worse than anyone else alive, but when we look around we discover that is surely not so. And we don't know, any of us, what is yet to happen in this life. I once read that "No one is immune to anything that can happen to man." It is how we deal with tragedy that matters, we've always been told. I believe that. I tried to always look to other overcomers as we journeyed. If you are one of those who has or is triumphing over incredible trials, thank you. March strong. I salute you. May our Twelve of Hearts speak to yours.

PART ONE

There is no twelve of hearts, you say?
It isn't in the deck to play?
The kings and queens and jacks are there,
And other numbers, everywhere...
But just as the marchers play their horns,
And actors play their parts,
We bow our heads and pray our prayers
And play the twelve of hearts.

I never really knew a whole lot about card-playing growing up. My father-in-law loved a game of Setback or Hearts and occasionally persuaded me to play early in my marriage. It was great fun. At least I got familiar with the deck a bit, enough to know the cards and their values. I know there is no chance of being dealt a twelve of any suit from a traditional deck, so if you get one, something's awry. It reminds me a little of life. We arrive in innocence, find our place and our normalcy and often, if we're fortunate, a state of peace, contentment, and fulfillment. Joy, even! We get comfortable with the terrain of our lives. We think we know what to expect after a while, so if life deals us a strange card we don't always know what to do with it.

Chapter 1 As Normal a Childhood As Ever Was

Brush the cobwebs from the hours
and the dust from off each day,
For a tiny smiling cherub's come
into our lives to stay...

I wrote those words in August, 1975, when Teresa was a week old. She was rosy and beautiful, a doll in my arms and a praise in my heart. She was Tuesday's child, full of grace. She grew up with two dedicated if very amateur parents, an energetic, fun-loving, risk-taking younger sister, aunts, uncles, cousins, and several neighborhood playmates. She was easy to love and a delightful companion with whom to visit and revisit childhood. She was straight and sturdy and the very picture of health.

Teresa adored her grandparents on both sides of the family and visited them often. She fished at the pond in the country, rode in Granddaddy Henry's wheelbarrow, and ate French fries late at night with her Aunt Fay. She and her sister played store with trinkets and change provided by Grandma Tulie and romped with the Power cousins, Mark, John, Robert, and Margaret, whenever they could visit. Teresa amazed us later in her life with the clear memory of her childhood years and the minutest details about things that happened. Some things we had forgotten until she brought them up. (Power cousins, she never forgot you shooting fireworks one holiday and setting the field afire at the side of the house.)

She was the first granddaughter of her Edwards grandparents and they delighted in her. At their house she learned about vegetable gardening as a family endeavor. Granddaddy Joe and Grandma Clara gave her the first tricycle, first wagon, and first bicycle that she owned. She was especially happy when the other Edwards grandchildren (J.K. and Ann) and she and her sister Melinda could spend the night there together. Christmas Eves we celebrated at their house and Granddaddy Joe would send us out to ride around town in the car after dinner "so

Santy Claus could come." When we got back, the tree would be aglow and gifts spilling out from under.

Teresa loved all animals: dogs, cats, birds, fishes, turtles, goats, pigs, rodents... Once when she was about five years old, Melinda came into the kitchen from outside and announced in her important almost three-year-old voice, "Teweesa gots a wat." I thought, "Oh, no, I hope it's not dead," then "Oh, no, I hope it's not alive." When I got outside to investigate, she held in her two hands a blind little ground mole with a pointed nose and she was stroking it lovingly, looking into its little face as if she had found a rare, valuable treasure. I had to explain that their dad would not love it so much, as it was making tunnels in the lawn along with its brothers and sisters, but that we would relocate it to a better place. They were okay with it making a comfortable move to the woods behind our house.

Our poodle Taffy was the puppy that set our girls up to love dogs into their adult lives, being the first pet that we kept close to us, inside the house, almost every minute of the day and night. Our outside cats Muffin and Pierre, then Charlie (who was rescued by Teresa) urged her into a love for felines as well. She kept a dog for nearly all of her adult life and a cat for many of those years too.

Teresa took gymnastic lessons and swimming lessons, roller skated, rode horses, was a junior cheerleader for a community football team, pedaled her bicycle to piano lessons, took part in almost all of our church's activities, and played cello in the school orchestra program. In her second grade music production, she danced as Cinderella in a blue taffeta dress I had fashioned for that purpose and when I look at the pictures of that now, I treasure that event as a symbol of much that was right and fun about a little girl growing up. She had several good neighborhood friends, Monica, April and Kathleen, with whom to share adventures. She found her upper elementary school niche in competitive dance – clogging. She was part of a team that traveled, and one of the highlights of those days before her diagnosis was dancing with her team on the stage of the Grand Ole Opry in Nashville.

Teresa was interested in everybody – family, friends, acquaintances – and wanted to know as much as she could about them. Some would call that trait "nosy." She had a friend named Kerry who became her best friend in late elementary school and early adolescence. Kerry was a bubbly petite ball of dance and energy, a friend with whom

Teresa shared the dreams and angst of that tilting world of tween and teen. Teresa loved television. She adored celebrations, holidays, picnics, spend-the-nights, family dinners, parades, Halloween, Thanksgiving, Christmas, Easter, July 4th, church socials, proms, weddings, birthdays (hers and everyone else's). She loved to make plans. She was always "looking forward to..." She had about as normal a childhood as I suppose there ever was.

While Teresa was full of plans, dreams, and enthusiasm for all that her life promised, she had a reserve about her too, even as a child, a thoughtfulness and quietness in her spirit that would sustain her throughout the hard times that she would face. That quiet spirit, her bright smile, an interest in others and their activities, that "looking forward" attitude, an almost uncontrollable laughter when she found something really funny, an incredible memory for every fun thing or place she ever experienced, and a love of glamour and glitz which she acquired as a teenager and young adult became some of her trademark personality traits.

We think we know how much we love our children. We tell them often of our love for them. We bring the best that we know to the task of raising them. We speak of our love for them to others with whom we share our lives in the workplace, in our extended families, in the church, in the community. But I now believe that none of us ever really feels how much we love a child or value his/her life until we are told that the promise of that life may not be fulfilled in the way we always dreamed it would be. This realization brings a multi-dimensional pain to mix with the joy of life, yielding an acute, heightened awareness of living – and dying – which leaves one changed in very nearly indescribable ways. Such was my "twelve of hearts."

It was the day before her twelfth birthday, August 11, 1987, when we learned that Teresa was not physically well. We had taken her faithfully through the years for those well-child physicals. She had a slight heart murmur when she was ten, but we were told by our pediatrician at the time that it was insignificant, that many children had one. Then in the summer of 1987, the nurse practitioner at our family practice detected a harsh systolic murmur in her exam. Looking back, I realize Teresa did tire easily, never being able to run too very far or hike any distance uphill. I remember that she had trouble finishing the physical fitness test in sixth grade P.E. but she did it – exhausted after.

Our wise nurse who detected the murmur that summer suggested we see a pediatric cardiologist. There was not one in our city at the time so we were sent to see a doctor in Charlotte, NC that August. After numerous tests, her father and I were called into a small room to engage in a conversation that went a little like this:

"Your daughter has hypertrophic cardiomyopathy."

"What exactly is that?"

"It's a thickening and stiffening of the heart muscle. It makes it difficult for the heart to fill and to relax. Some patients have this and have virtually no symptoms and few problems. Sometimes it is obstructive, but hers is not. Her whole heart is extremely enlarged, however."

"What does this mean for her? In the way of lifestyle changes? In longevity?"

"It's hard to say. I think she should stop clogging immediately. It's serious. It's hard to say what direction it will take with a child, but hers seems very advanced. Sometimes young athletes die suddenly from this. I'm sorry..."

I began to feel that there was not enough air in my lungs, in the room, or in the world for me to breathe. I remember looking into my husband's face and seeing the grief and disbelief there. Terry was able to weep that night when we returned home, to pour himself out. I was paralyzed, and just when I knew I needed momentum for a long, long journey.

Chapter 2 In Everything Give Thanks

It **has** been a long, long journey since Teresa's precious life became to me as "a candle in the wind." On this day in 1998 as I sit at my computer it has been eleven years since that day our world changed so dramatically and began to turn in a strange new direction. On that day of her grim diagnosis, I recall asking the doctor from somewhere deep inside the cavern of my disbelief, maybe mostly talking aloud to myself, "How will we ever tell her this?"

The doctor, having heard, replied, "Don't tell her. She does not have to know. Let her live her life. Yes, there are restrictions, but you don't need to tell her yet about the seriousness of this." I was still at the stage of my life that I believed every single word that a doctor said to me, about myself and about anyone I entrusted into his care. My two great uncles, whom I never knew, were doctors, having taken care of my parents and several of my older siblings. Their names, Uncle Gene and Uncle Raiford, were revered in our household. Looking back, I think Teresa's doctor's advice may not have been the best that day, but we never questioned that we would try to follow it. We did not anticipate how she would eventually learn the gravity of her diagnosis.

So we did not tell Teresa for a long time how sick she could become or that there was a chance of a sudden lethal arrhythmia. We told almost no one, in fact, of how very serious it was, for fear it would get back to her. I can still feel what I felt in those first days, that numbing, paralyzing depression, the sense of tragedy and loss, grief and mourning, and the constant fear, always with me. I felt like a robot, moving through the days, weeks, and months. I could barely put one foot before the other. I moved mechanically to keep our girls fed, in school, myself and Terry off to work. "You do have this severe heart murmur, Teresa, and it keeps you from doing some of the things you used to." That's all she knew and mostly all anyone knew except for Terry and me, the doctors, and a trusted few in our workplaces. Inside of ourselves, we were dying. I can't describe the agony of our loss, both actual for her lifestyle in the present, and for all of the imaginings toward what the future would be like. A sudden death? Growing fatigue?

Chest and/or other pain? A struggle for breath? The pain and disability of a heart attack? A stroke? A pharmacy of medicine? Other horrid scenarios we had not even heard about? None or all of that?

Once past those early days, while still doing daily battle with the darkness, I sought to cup my hands, to drape my very life around that flame that was her life, to keep it burning brightly. I wanted to prepare myself to fight for her life and for the quality of her life in any arena of the world. Our fight led us to learn medical terminology we had never imagined. We met countless medical experts with brilliant minds and various personalities. I could tell you about a dozen drugs that work for various stages of her heart disease. I could tell you of my search for information and a dozen times I did and did not find it. I can conjure multiple adjectives that tell you how it feels when one's heart is broken, physically and emotionally. I could try, futilely probably, to explain helplessness.

But as I contemplate our twelve of hearts, in the list of lessons learned and life experienced, one of the most important is from the Apostle Paul when he told us in I Thessalonians 5:18 "In everything give thanks..." As I examined my life and that of my family while moving beyond those early days, into the months and years of Teresa's adolescence, I decided we would never make it through without finding thankfulness in every single place we could. Some of them are the same kinds of things you are thankful for as you look around your own life. Some of them may be a little different.

One of the first things I found when I set out purposefully to be thankful was the twelve years of active childhood that Teresa had had. I began to realize on that day of her diagnosis how much we had taken for granted, how much each of us takes for granted. The happy little face staring out of those photographs through the years knew nothing of the limitations that lay ahead. She would always have her memories of whirling around the skating rink, of cheering with her sister for one of the community football league teams, of riding the cantankerous Frosty in a horse show, and of dancing on the stage of the Grand Old Opry with her dance team. After Teresa's diagnosis and her cardiologist cautioned her against strenuous physical exercise, she could no longer dance, a tremendous disappointment to her. When that happened, Chris and Dina Davis, her dance instructors, gave her the job of Sound Technician so that she could continue to travel with her team. What a gift that was to her. I continue to be thankful for the ones God puts in our path to enhance our strengths, to push us into those larger selves.

I began to be thankful that, when it became necessary, we learned to redefine "normal." There was a children's book when the girls were tiny about a rabbit named Leo the Lop. Leo wanted to have normal ears instead of the ones that hung down. He tried various tricks to fashion himself some ordinary rabbit ears, including hanging upside down by his feet. Then he finally accepted that lop ears were normal for him. Everyone has to adjust in some ways to find his/her own normal sometimes. No, it was not always easy for her, but Teresa began to accept, in those initial years, some things as normal for her: low blood pressure, some shortness of breath, a reduced stamina, and some medications that further increased her fatigue. Also normal for her, though, were a loving, lovable, steady disposition, the constant support of family and friends, an amazing wonderment and appreciation for the small blessings of life, and an abiding faith in the One who holds the future. She adjusted. She continued her regular school attendance, her new job with the dance team, and her interaction with family and friends. We are thankful for those normals and for the strength she had for so long to maintain an adjusted normal physical lifestyle. She could easily have been resentful of the active physical lifestyle of others she saw around her.

When Teresa became a teenager, we enrolled her in a local modeling school which taught young women self-assurance, current fashion and makeup techniques, and how to put your best foot forward, as well as providing opportunities for storefront modeling and photography shoots. She loved this. She continued until early adolescence playing cello in the school orchestra. She learned to drive at the permitted age and not having experienced any syncope with the heart disease, she drove to school and anywhere else she needed to go. With the encouragement of Lynn Eargle, our pastor's wife, we surprised her with a sixteenth birthday party attended by church and school friends.

She went with our church youth group on many of their excursions. Her dad and I often went along on those that were a distance away. She participated in several of the drama productions that our youth group at church performed. We have a videotape of her in a musical performed by some of the college/career group after she got her defibrillator but before her health began to deteriorate further. As I remember, she played the character of a girl who stood up for someone whose life was off-track, someone who could easily be judged as unworthy by others. Little did she know that the circumstances of her real life would become an inspiration for many who would observe them and God's work in the midst of them and be changed. Teresa loved the Lord, Oakwood Church, its people, its ministers, and its ministries her whole life. All of these experiences gave her a sense of belonging, of normalcy, despite her physical limitations.

I began to realize how thankful we should be for a family that was staunch in their support of us. I could list a dozen ways that the hearts of various members of our extended families have been broken through the years. There have been sicknesses, divorces, depression, unemployment, tragedy, and misunderstandings, as there have been in nearly every family. But never was there a time when we did not feel loved by them. Teresa was named for her father and for her aunt, my only sister, who never had children of her own. How Fay rejoiced in her life! I am thankful for another daughter whose life I celebrate. Melinda reached into some dark, dreary places to retrieve our sense of humor and our optimism for us when we had misplaced them. I remember when I first told her about the seriousness of Teresa's illness, of telling her about certain possible complications and that there was a ten percent chance of sudden death from a lethal arrhythmia. Her reply: "To me that means there is a ninety percent chance she won't have one." I pray there is a one hundred percent chance that she knows how much her dad and I have loved her throughout these long hard years, too.

I remain thankful for my own health and that of my husband. We would gladly have swapped our own good health for her diagnosis if that had been possible. While it would be a dark, dark lie to say that we understand why she had to have this illness, we always tried to trust God's plan. Teresa depended on us, not only as a child but into her adult life. What if we had had health issues as well? It is a blessing that we have been well physically through the years. This heart disease sometimes occurs in families. So far it has not been found in any other family members.

I am thankful for the supportive workplace I enjoyed during my working career with Lexington School District One. I had a wonderful administration, good health insurance, and a fair leave policy. I had precious friends at both of the schools I served as media specialist during these tough personal times. My Christian friend Edna was a rock on whom I leaned personally, professionally, and spiritually in good times and bad and from whom I learned so very much about how to look at the life we have been given and how to live it. To her I could tell anything and it would come back to me uniquely blessed. My lively friend and coworker Patty experienced my broken heart at another stage of Teresa's disease. Tenderhearted and compassionate, she also knew when and how to stop me from pitying myself and Teresa too much and turn me toward grabbing hold once again. There were five Christian ladies who worked as library assistants with me at various times during the White Knoll Middle School years and who were invaluable in my professional and personal life: Sandra, Karen, Cerese, Lori, and Wanda. Contact with hundreds of students through the years kept my mind, hands, and heart busy and kept me in touch with a reality as only children and young adolescents experience it.

Likewise, Terry and Teresa had the good fortune to work with people who showed their love and support in immeasurable ways. Teresa got her first job in a medical office during high school and enjoyed working there, filing, answering phones, getting to know the medical records personnel. Later she got work at a law office and continued working there throughout college and after. Her employers appreciated the job Teresa did for them and held a place for her throughout the hard times for as long as she was able to work. Her supervisor Sundai became a big sister who remained that even when their career paths separated. Terry's coworkers were truly his brothers and sisters and he made valued, irreplaceable friendships in his workplace and his loyal customer base there, as well as in our church and community.

The words of a doctor on August 11, 1987 changed the life of a family forever. I think disease is never easy. When it is a beloved child, it is beyond devastating. What we all must remember is that none of us is guaranteed tomorrow. We are all "candles in the wind" and must celebrate the life we have been given. And if we are doing whatever God has given us to do, the promise of our life **is** being fulfilled in the way that He intended.

Chapter 3 More Thanksgiving... and Supplication

I began to pray and give thanks early on for every doctor, nurse, researcher, technician, nutritionist, therapist, scheduler, record-keeper, pharmacist, chaplain, insurance agent, patient liaison, housekeeper, volunteer, social worker, food service worker, transporter, and the list could continue... in the medical field who would ever help us and Teresa. There is no job in their realm that I do not appreciate. After our cardiologist in Charlotte diagnosed Teresa's problem, he told us that if we wanted to talk to the man who probably knew more than anyone in the world about hypertrophic cardiomyopathy, to go to the National Institutes of Health in Bethesda, Maryland and see Dr. Barry Maron. We began to journey there about every six months. Teresa was seen there for a number of years throughout her adolescence. When Dr. Maron moved on to another facility, we saw Dr. Lameh Fananapazir and his associates there. We found Dr. John Beard, a cardiologist in Columbia, to keep up with Teresa locally. Dr. Henry Martin was her doctor at our local family practice. Eventually the journey led to consultations at Duke and then to MUSC in Charleston. Among our many medical professionals we found a range of personalities, nationalities, and some differences of opinion, but with few exceptions there was a compassionate spirit of helpfulness and a commitment to doing the right thing.

While being treated at NIH we met a family named Antrim. The hypertrophic cardiomyopathy that these family members had ran in their family; a number of family members had it. While Teresa's disease did not appear to be genetic, this family was still a great support to us when we met them in Bethesda. They were participating in some of the clinical trials there that were being developed to better understand the cardiomyopathy and to improve treatment in those who had the disease. A people of faith, they freely shared their experiences and were continuing to live their lives as fully as possible. I have never forgotten them and the good they were to us during this time and I remain thankful for them.

It was at one of her visits to NIH that Teresa found out how serious her heart condition really was. The attending physician had not gotten the word that she had not been given the whole story. He spilled out enough of the prognosis that we had to finish telling her what we knew about the heart disease. It stunned her and I remember how difficult the trip home was from that visit. Once back at home, after an initial bout with disbelief and disappointment and "what if's" her indomitable spirit took over once again and she grabbed hold.

I am thankful that:

"Hope is the thing with feathers, that perches in the soul,

And sings the tune without the words, and never stops, at all."

Emily Dickinson said that a long time ago. Hope tends to get lost in the midst of sadness, sickness, and discouragement. We mustn't let it. In the many years since Teresa was diagnosed, there have been medical miracles accomplished in so many fields of research. I believe there is hope out there for even the worst of our ailments, whether of the body, mind, or spirit. I've also heard it said that we all need something to love, something to do, and something to hope for. We tried to give Teresa all of those things. Even now, when someone I know gets a seemingly grim diagnosis, I try to remind them of what the scientists are learning every day. Think of all the things that seemed hopeless such a short while ago!

I am thankful to have learned that fear and pity (not to be confused with caution and compassion) can be crippling emotions. In November of 1996 Teresa had a mild stroke late one evening when she was spending the night away from home. I can still feel what I felt when the call came: a numbing fear that took my breath and vacuumed up my spirit and robbed me of energy and coherence. I remember asking myself when I saw her arm hanging limply down from the ambulance gurney, "How will she ever dry her hair again?" "Will she even be able to pour a glass of milk or pet the cat or walk outside?" "How will she use the computer keyboard she counts on?" I recall begging for God's help.

Teresa's stroke was mild – God brought her back to us nearly 100% intact from that medical crisis, making me ashamed of my fear that night. But it is hard to overcome such a feeling of fear with your heart even when your mind has learned it. My heart still "leaps up" – but not with joy - when the phone rings late at night. It is good to remember with Shakespeare's Caesar that "Cowards die many times before their deaths; the valiant never taste of death but once." Regarding pity: Teresa wanted to live her life as a regular, normal person, as do most who are ill or handicapped in any way. Pity can keep them from doing that. I have had numerous pity picnics for myself. (I found out I could cry fairly loudly, without anyone hearing, in the bathtub late at night if I ran the water hard enough.) On the other hand, Teresa's life and ours have been blessed repeatedly by the kindness of compassionate people. We have learned, in turn, how to show compassion instead of pity whenever possible. **And** to remember that while we suffer, there are others out there with problems that are important, seemingly insurmountable to them as well.

I am thankful for a cat named Charlie. He came to us through Teresa when she was twenty-one years old. He had been hurt so badly in an accident that nobody thought he would live but a few more breaths. His face was gaping and he had lost all use of one leg. Our Teresa persuaded a veterinarian to fix him up and she brought him home. In this case, "Hope was the thing with fur the color of midnight that perched in our laundry room ready to leap onto our shoulders every time the door opened, purring a song of love and thanksgiving that never stopped at all." Charlie fooled all the skeptics. He got well enough to present a handsome face to the world and to walk with scarcely a limp on a leg that had initially been doomed for amputation. Charlie, though he lived his life out with us (his grandparents!), was Teresa's cat and a hero of sorts, a role model from which we can all learn. He made a fine parallel to Teresa. She never "dragged her paw" or "exploited her wound" either. She smiled all through the years. She went to school and work and life every minute she could possibly attend. She was Charlie's person, and ours.

In every single thing give thanks? Then I suppose I must give thanks for an incident that occurred in Teresa's early adult life. She had gone into atrial fibrillation and various medications and five cardioversions could not keep her out of it. (Part of her heart quivered instead of beating rhythmically.) Her stamina diminished so that she could not walk any distance at all without stopping. The doctor approved a handicapped parking placard which she began to use when she was especially fatigued. Once when she returned to her car at a mall, she had received a handwritten rebuke on her windshield, shaming her for parking in a handicapped parking space with someone else's parking pass, thus keeping a real handicapped person from using the space. My heart flooded with rage upon reading this scathing epistle which she brought to me along with a face etched with hurt and disbelief. I wanted to call someone, to write someone, to go back there and find the writer and drag the person with me to the medical records office and open a young woman's record now six inches thick and explain things. I understood a little of how crimes of rage can happen. But I also began to understand a little bit better the words of the Christ: "Father, forgive them, for they know not what they do," Luke 23:34 (KJV) and "Judge not, that ye be not judged." Matthew 7:1-3 (KJV) Teresa's handicap was not a readily visible one. Perhaps the person thought himself/herself a good citizen in making such a reprimand? But I vowed then to adhere more closely to the well-known Native American advice: "Never judge a man until you have walked a mile in his moccasins." We never know what problems people have. I am trying to be thankful to have that lesson reinforced, albeit it in such a bitter way.

I am thankful for a boy of thirteen with, as the song says, "starlight in his eyes" who found Teresa when she was also thirteen and never let go of her. He would love her through orchestra class, math class, computer class, church youth group trips, ballgames, two proms, their high school graduation, every holiday with our family and his, visits to multiple doctors, numerous hospitalizations, the news that she would someday need a heart transplant, her struggle to finish her associate's degree at a local technical college, and every other event of significance (more to come in future chapters about their life together) in both of their lives. Bradley Taylor was her "someone to love" on this earth in that special way. He knew her diagnosis and prognosis and that she and he might struggle, but he persevered in his love for her, and she for him.

Finally, but certainly not last in significance, we are thankful that the Christian church, when it operates by the principles upon which it was founded, is more than just a steeple against the sky. When I think of my church, I see Chris and Cecil and Gail and Jerry visiting in a hospital room every time we had to have one. I hear Janie crying God's tears for us. I hear Beverly and Carolyn and Ginger and Sylvia and countless others taking the prayers we couldn't even pray and mixing them with their own and offering them to Him. I can taste Penny's potato soup and ham while she let me spew my deepest feelings out to her. I can feel the hugs of young people and the concern of my Sunday School sisters whose child Teresa became in their own hearts during those hardest of times. I see Becky and Gayle, two young career women friends of Teresa's, trying countless wedding dresses on her and never getting impatient even when they had to stop for dizziness and breathlessness and "I can't do anymore today." I see Peggy planning a wedding shower and Penny (along with more ladies than I can name) organizing, planning, and preparing a wedding reception that helped make her dreams come true on May 23, 1998 when she married her friend of nearly ten years. God's goodness surely poured into our lives through these our friends in these best and worst of times.

So many prayers went up for Teresa after we eventually began to tell our church and other friends about her diagnosis. I believed in my heart that one morning God was going to look around at his band of angels and say something like, "Let's see... Teresa Edwards ... I've heard her name over and over. I think I'll fix her heart today." While I would have cheerfully laid down my life at any moment for Teresa to have a healthy heart, I would not have swapped one hour or one minute of her life for any other person she could have been. I felt that someday she would get a new physical heart and I prayed toward that possibility if she ever became so sick as to need it. But I knew that she would still have the heart of her that mattered most, that strong, wonderful, smiling spirit deep inside of her.

"...Count it all joy...!" James 1: 2 (KJV)

PART TWO

1999 –

I wrote this poem one night as I sat with Teresa during an in-hospital stay at the National Institutes of Health. Teresa was doing better than I was by far. I knew I had to make a conscious effort to be joyful, not sorrowful. I never wanted her memories at any stage to be viewed through my sadness and despair even though I often felt those two emotions. Blessed indeed are those who find joy as a companion...

I danced with Joy
Even when Sorrow played the tunes,
and Joy held me fast
Until the echoes of the pain
which sorrow piped...
were past.
And if It comes to play again
I'll dance with Joy still,
For Sorrow only has the night
But Joy claims the morning.

Based on Psalm 30: 5 and 11

Chapter 4 Fulfilled Dreams Despite the Struggles

After her diagnosis and throughout her adolescence Teresa led what I think of as a carefully tended, limited, but as full of normal life as she and we could make it. She did not take a lot of medicines early on, just a beta blocker that slowed her heart rate somewhat, as it tended to race at times. She was fatigued, yes, due to the inefficient heart muscle and the beta blocker, but overall was able to guardedly enjoy a quality of life as a teenager for which we remain thankful.

In her early adulthood, Teresa continued to wring all the quality of life that was possible from each day. During her early twenties, we could see her energy diminishing gradually. She would go for a period of weeks and sometimes a few months without any major problems, and then she would notice that her breath was more labored or her stamina lessened. Her need for medical care was fairly constant. She would go into atrial fibrillation (her heart in that area quivering instead of beating regularly) but would sometimes come out and back into sinus rhythm on her own. After that stroke in 1996 she began to take the blood thinner Coumadin. She started to need drugs for the atrial fib. A drug would work for a while and then she would go out of rhythm again. She was cardioverted five times. She was placed on a regimen of drugs to help her heart pump better too.

An electrophysiology study was done in 1997 that determined there was a potentially dangerous arrhythmia in Teresa's heart and a definite need for an ICD (Implanted Cardiac Defibrillator). She received the Guardian Angel in March of 1997 at Providence Hospital. When she went into the hospital for that surgery, one of the nurses asked me if we wanted a May Day called if she arrested, that she had about the most aberrant "rhythm" she had ever observed on the monitors they used to observe patients. Without hesitation, I replied, "We want you to do every single thing you know to do to save her life." Teresa did not have problems with her arrhythmia during that hospital stay, but the night after the ICD was implanted, she developed a hematoma the size of a baseball at the surgery site and had to go back into surgery to remedy that the next morning. After several days in the hospital, though, she was back at home and resuming all of the tasks she could manage.

During that hospital stay at Providence Teresa met a patient named Carl Farmer. Carl had struggled for a long time with his weight, his heart, and a number of medical conditions. A Christian man, he continued to look up and encouraged others to do so. He wrote poetry and some of his verses inspired us during that time and we tried to keep up with Carl for a long time after, exchanging Christmas cards and writing letters. His mother Nancy was traveling the journey with him and we felt drawn to them as both of our cases advanced.

While the ICD was a protection against sudden cardiac arrest, after Teresa had it implanted in her chest, there were things she could not do. Any strong magnetic field had the potential to interfere with it. Amusement rides were off-limits. She had loved to stand with Bradley when he tinkered with car engines and she could no longer do that. She would try to exercise with him at the rec center, but that stopped when her heart rate soared one night when she was walking around the gym and the device shocked her three consecutive times. Another night a house fire occurred at the home of a friend of Melinda's. We went there to see what we could do. Teresa insisted she wanted to come too. Once there, the ICD began to discharge, not once, but five times. Terry grabbed her up in his arms and he received the shocks too as he carried her away from the fire truck, thinking it might be the magnetic fields surrounding it. Her ICD was later adjusted for the fast rate it was reading due to her atrial fibrillation, but she never felt secure in such situations again. The device terrified her. The defibrillator nurses at the Heart Center were wonderful to her, and if it had not been for their encouragement and reassurance Teresa could have easily given in to some major depression and despair.

She got a medic alert bracelet that showed her medical information including the heart condition, the drugs she was taking, the ICD of course, and contact information for people to be notified if there was a problem. This was another safeguard that the medical professionals suggested, particularly after the ICD was implanted. Teresa wore this early on, then I think she decided it called too much attention to her condition, and while we fussed about it, there were some things she would not give in to. The bracelet was sometimes carried in her purse instead of worn on her arm.

Despite the defibrillator and her regimen of heart rhythm/rate, anticoagulant, and heart failure drugs, Teresa continued to nurture the normal in her days. She was maintaining a reduced-energy lifestyle but giving 100 percent of the energy she did have to the things she still enjoyed and could accomplish. She had been struggling to finish her degree from Midlands Technical College. The stroke had rendered her, while thankfully not paralyzed, slightly weaker in her left arm and hand and she needed to type 60 words a minute as I recall to make it out of one of her classes. She practiced and practiced and finally met that goal with the assistance of her teachers at the school. Graduating with her Associate Degree in Office Systems Technology was quite an achievement in her life and served her well in the workforce later.

One day as we were sitting at the SC Heart Center waiting for her to be seen by the doctor, she said, "I have to get away from here in plenty of time today. I think Bradley is giving me a ring tonight." While I should not have been surprised at this after nine years, I **was** surprised and that amused her so. She seemed so very, very happy at the impending engagement and at surprising me with the announcement at the doctor's office.

Their engagement did in fact commence that night, and Teresa entered the blissful if stressful adventure of making those plans. Shopping for the dress, choosing a photographer, engaging through my friend Susan a wonderful group of string musicians, choosing things for her gift registry... all of this thrilled her. Melinda was to serve as her maid of honor, her cousin Ann and her friends Gayle and Becky as bridesmaids. Our pastor's five-year-old daughter would be Teresa's flower girl and the little son of one of Teresa's coworkers at the medical office where she had worked as a teen agreed to be the ring bearer. Bradley's brothers, Melinda's boyfriend, and Teresa's cousin J.K., along with Bradley's dad as best man completed the wedding party. Her friend Gayle was going to serve double duty by also directing the wedding and Teresa was so thankful for that direction.

I remember on Teresa and Bradley's wedding day that Martin, Bradley's brother, opened up his tuxedo duds and found that he had been given two left shoes to wear. He cheerfully jammed them on and was planning to bear up to this discomfort. Gayle found out in time to get the wrong shoe swapped out – she could meet any challenge it seemed. Becky was my good friend Penny's daughter, and Penny had approached the ladies of our church about Teresa's wedding reception and got an overwhelming response from those who wanted to plan and prepare the reception (more later in my Penny chapter). Teresa was given wonderful showers by friends and family. She was exhausted so much of the time but remained committed to her plans and with the help and enthusiasm of so, so many she achieved her dream of reaching the altar with Bradley. Terry gave the bride away in a nearly full church on May 23, 1998. The vows had scarcely started before I began to cry and the bridesmaids began to puddle as well. We could scarcely believe how far she and we had come.

Chapter 5 Simple Joys

Bradley's grandfather and grandmother Miller (Gee-Pa and Gee-Ma) gave to him a piece of family property in the country and this is where Teresa and Bradley began their married life. They were about fourteen miles from us and we continued to see them often. We visited them there and they came our way for church and other visits. Their home was snug and comfortable. Teresa didn't have lots of money, but she had taken great delight in carefully planning each bedspread, pillow, picture, plant, rug, mirror, and decorative object that she put there. You could feel the peace in her den and kitchen where she had her braided rug under the table, her prized birdhouses around the walls and flowers on the table. When I asked one day where some item was in her kitchen, she said, "You know, Ma, same place they are at your house: in the cupboard above the stove." She loved to keep house.

The day after she married Bradley, Teresa went to the nearby flea market and came back with a little Chihuahua puppy the size of a large coffee mug. As she deposited him on my lap, she said, "I had to have him, Ma. Will you keep him for me while I go on my honeymoon?" I could not deny her anything in those days, so we made a place for little Zack in our house for a while and he got to know Taffy, our aging poodle, and Charlie the cat who still lived with us. He was the most hyper thing I had ever encountered, that Zack, all wriggle and yap. It was almost as if Teresa had to have the most active dog breed out there to make up for the energy she sometimes lacked. We loved Zack for the space of about a week and then he went to Teresa and Bradley to become the most fiercely protective, most highly pampered prince of a lap dog ever to gnaw bones. Teresa called him her "high energy lover boy." He got something from the grocery store almost every time she went and they left a radio playing for him when they went out. They really tried not to, but eventually they surrendered a place on their bed for him to sleep at night and he had to have a bone and a blanket of his own to burrow under before he could settle in. I believe God gave this little dog to Teresa to get her through some of her sickest days. Zack didn't always seem to understand when she felt so very bad, too bad to talk and hug and play so much with him, but she never, ever stopped being his person to love.

Teresa rescued another cat after she married too. She went out on her back deck one day and was greeted by this poor little bag of bones with no tail. It meowed and meowed until Teresa couldn't stand it. She thought its tail had been severed in an accident and she knew it definitely had had very little to eat from the time it was born. She began to feed it and it worked its way into her heart and finally into her house. Once when she was feeding this adopted one outside she looked up to see several other cats (also tailless!) looking her way. She was glad at least to find out that her cat had not been traumatized in a tail-severing accident - it had inherited that designer look. They named this one Shelby and while her early life was full of suffering, including the expensive birth of one kitten that she later lost, she gradually became a feline queen who lived more than comfortably in the Taylor household for a time.

Besides her marriage and family, her home and her animals, Teresa enjoyed crafts, fishing, her church, her part-time job, and vacationing at the beach and the mountains. And she loved shopping and eating out! She had taken a cake decorating class before marrying and she continued to bake cakes. She could devise almost any scene on top of a cake. Clowns, flowers, graduating seniors, Dalmatians, trucks, cars, and fishermen appeared on some of her creations. Her greatest delight was not in the money she earned, but in the pleasure of the recipient. Always she would ask, "Do you think they liked it?" One word of praise or affirmation would motivate her for a long time.

One Christmas she made Santa Clauses out of Clorox bottles and yarn. She could not keep up with the demand. Friends and acquaintances who bought them told me long afterward that they hung them every Christmas for years and years. Her love of crafts had started much earlier. I recall that she had made Easter bunnies out of dish cloths while she was in the hospital getting her defibrillator. Several of the staff wanted them. I can remember scouring the local variety stores for just the right bath cloths, towels, and ribbons to bring to her in the hospital. She sat there among the tubes and wires and "created."

While she could no longer stand by while Bradley worked on those car engines, fishing was one thing she could share with him. She was ready to go to the dock or the pond bank almost any time if the fishing was good. She was especially happy if Bradley and her dad went along and if I came too and brought a picnic basket that was an added bonus. Bradley's family enjoyed getting together and she was happy to get to attend those occasions with him. Bradley helped her with housework and they watched lots of movies on television. She began to read more than she ever had before.

Teresa never left her home church. She and Bradley visited churches closer to home but she never moved her membership. It was a 14-mile drive for her, but she continued to come to church with us in those days, bringing Bradley with her. I would prepare lunch for all of us at my house afterward, a tradition we kept up throughout the years. As her diet became more and more complicated I struggled and often felt that I had not provided the most appetizing meals but we continued to use that time to be together as a family. Long after Melinda had moved out, she continued to come on Sundays too so that she could see Teresa and Bradley.

Teresa still worked as she was able. She had aspired to something in a medical field when she was a teenager, but knowing that she might lack the stamina for that, she had pursued and received that degree in Office Systems Technology. She was dependable and organized and willing to learn new things. Jim Sketo, of Rick Hall and Lexington Titles, taught her how to read plats "like an architect" as he described it. She learned so much in that office and made lifelong friends when she joined Sundai, Michelle, Laurie, Carolyn, and Kathy there, then others who came on through the years. The accountant John who had an office in the same building also had work for Teresa during tax season some years. He and his wife Trish were good to her, knowing that there were good days and bad for her. She was good at concealing the bad, though, choosing instead when someone asked how she was, to smile and answer, "Fine," even after she became really limited in what she could do. She remained close to her friends in the office during her illness. Truly she did dance with joy, even when sorrow appeared to be playing more and more of the tunes.

Teresa continued to love all holidays with the delight of a child. She tried never to miss the Macy's Thanksgiving Day parade on TV which ushered in the Christmas season for her. She was awed by the Christmas celebrations held in our community, among them the "Singing Christmas Tree" and "This Man Called Jesus." She especially enjoyed inviting

Bradley's grandmother or great-grandmother to those. Her dad played the part of Jesus in the Easter pageant at our church some years, and she always looked forward to that. Everyone's birthday deserved a celebration and the more family and friends that could attend, the better. One of her most frequently asked questions was, "What are we doing for - and she would name some holiday - July 4th, Memorial Day, Father's Day, etc.?" If we ever had to tell her that some family member could not make it, she always asked, "Why NOT?" She could get a little indignant about poor attendance!

Teresa was all about vacations, too. She was able to make at least two trips to the beach and one to the mountains during those years between her defibrillator hospitalization and her end stage heart failure. She was good at planning and packing – or directing the packing - for all of this. If it was too hot she could not breathe as well or walk any distance to speak of. Flatter ground at the beach was good if the weather was not too hot. Cooler temperatures in the mountains were wonderful if the hills were not too steep. More than once Bradley would piggyback her from one place to another. She had an incredible memory for the details of every place she ever vacationed and it was always a delight for the rest of us to be reminded of something she would pull out of her mind and heart about a trip somewhere in the past.

As I look back at those (relatively) tranquil months in her life and her health, it reinforces the thought that there is so much contentment to be had in simplicity. Teresa wanted all she could get from life, but "all" to her were the simple joys mentioned here. None of us knew how elusive those simple pleasures were to become to her in the later months of her illness, but they were the memories she would cling to as she fought for her life in late 1999 and 2000.

Chapter 6 End of Road

"No more!"
I rage and shout and threaten to the sky.
"I'll tuck my head beneath
my heart
And die..."
"But no,"
He gently whispers back.
"This trial will teach you
How to grow and gain and give
And how
to live..."

I've thought often through the years about the colors assigned to various emotions or character traits. We've heard about the yellow-bellied coward, seeing red, being green with envy, in a blue mood, earning the Purple Heart, and assigning white to innocence or purity and black to death, mourning, or evil, among others. But what is the color assigned to pain, physical and/or emotional? Mix a little yellow (fear), a little blue (sadness), some purple (courage), a measure of red (rage), perhaps some white (innocence) and just a speck of green (for envy, maybe, for one of the few times in all of Teresa's illness when she voiced, in the middle of a long, sleepless, breathless night, a wish that her life could be different). What does this combination equal on the artist's palette? Some shade of muddled grayish-brown, perhaps? Color the months of late 1999 and early 2000 that color.

What had occurred in Teresa's heart during the years was, according to a doctor's report, "a marked deterioration in left ventricular function and marked thinning of the septum." There had also been "replacement of myocardial tissue by scar tissue," setting her up for atrial and ventricular arrhythmias and a high risk of sudden death from these arrhythmias. Add to the fear of a sudden lethal arrhythmia her progressing heart failure symptoms and the picture was grim. But Teresa never focused on that as long as she could minimally function. It was when she began to lose even the most basic activities that she truly began to flounder, to suffer with a pain that threatened to defeat us all.

I've pondered often about how we made it through those next several months of struggle. The doctors were trying everything they knew. Dr. Beard and all of the staff at the South Carolina Heart Center we considered our friends as well as our medical "keepers." We had our other good friends and neighbors. I found a gift of note cards for my friend Penny once and the quote on them was something like, "It's good to have a friend, who, when I cry, she tastes tears." So many poured themselves into our suffering. And our family background helped us, as I am sure any strong family can attest to. I summarized our family tree a bit for Melinda on one of her birthdays when I wrote for her: If you feel a sense of family loyalty, you can know that Granddaddy Joe Edwards loved and kept up with everyone in his family (wife, children, grandchildren, cousins, uncles, aunts...) until the day he died. If you feel any stoicism to face hard times, thank the Mayers. They were hard-working, slow to anger, and not easily discouraged. If you feel a generosity of spirit and soft-heartedness for people and animals, thank the Parkers. They had both of those traits, as you've seen in your great aunt Nee-Nee, Aunt Ruth, and Grandma Tulie particularly. If you have a love of a good time, a tendency to be able to tell a good story, and the desire and ability to treat every person (prince or pauper) as a friend, thank Granddaddy Henry Power. I think God was probably letting some of these precious ones watch over all of us here during those dark days.

But while we had our medical community, our staunch friends at work, church, and in our neighborhood, and our strong family background, I know beyond all doubt that it was God's big hand on us that ultimately brought us through. He used many compassionate people and a good number of his angels, too, I'm sure. Too many things happened that were not coincidental or "just luck." It is difficult to think and write about some of these circumstances without weeping even now, but in the tellling I believe God is truly glorified. He had to have shown us what to do in so many instances and he had to have instilled in Teresa and in us some force that willed her to live. I believe that with my whole heart.

Teresa would call me during the months of summer in 1999 and say, "I can't breathe right, Ma" or "My stomach hurts just awful" or "I can't do anything anymore, it seems." Some days she felt dizzy or off-balance. She would seem to rally enough to do some small thing she longed to do, but then nearly collapse from the effort. When she came to our house, she would walk from the car through our kitchen door and head for the sofa in the den and stay there. I became increasingly alarmed by her stomach problems. I recall the exact day that I knew something was dreadfully wrong.

My fiftieth birthday was in October, 1999. Teresa so wanted to take me out to eat. She and Bradley, Terry, Melinda and I went over into Columbia to eat at the California Dreaming Restaurant there. She ate almost nothing, saying she felt full after a few bites. It was that day that I got her to admit that her digestive problem was more than an occasional stomachache. It was ongoing, every day, with nausea, bleeding from her colon and a feeling of fullness in her stomach almost all the time. She craved milk above any other food. She was scheduled to see the cardiologist for her increased shortness of breath the next day and we insisted that she mention these symptoms to him. She did, and Dr. Beard got her an appointment with a gastro doctor immediately. This doctor came out with more words to turn my blood to ice (a cliché that I totally understand now): "She has to have a colonoscopy as soon as possible. We need to know what is causing this fresh blood and the pain she is having."

Consider this procedure as not pleasant under usual circumstances. Compound it with heart failure and heart rhythm problems, the inability to hold down a normal meal, a gallon of prep solution that had to be drunk, and the fear of sedation during the procedure because of her heart trouble and the fear of not enough sedation to be able to endure it, and this was the situation Teresa faced. The first scheduled procedure was canceled at the last minute because she had not retained enough of the prep, but the second time they were able to complete it. They had said that there was a possibility that the heart's ejection fraction to her colon could be so low that it was causing some of these problems, but after the colonoscopy was over, the doctor came back with a diagnosis of ulcerative colitis. I was so thankful it was not cancer, as they had also feared it might be. I really didn't understand what ulcerative colitis was, but that was to be my next assignment.

I discovered that ulcerative colitis is one of the inflammatory bowel diseases and once it shows up, it hangs around. You always have it. It could become dormant for a while and usually it can be at least partially managed with medicine. They did not want to give Teresa the steroids usually prescribed for the condition because of the possibility of fluid retention, which she did not need with her weakened heart. They did give her some Asacol, another medicine, to take. She suffered terribly with pain for some time after the colonoscopy. Then, while not back to normal in a digestive sense, her system was somewhat soothed and she could eat a bit more than she could before. She kept her shortness of breath, her light-headedness, and her craving for milk and later, crushed ice.

Teresa wasn't working regularly by this time, but she wanted to work some and took on a couple of weeks' part-time work at her friend Sundai's office in December. She did not feel comfortable driving by this time, so I drove her over to Columbia for the hours she was to work. (I was off for Christmas break.) Teresa didn't have the strength for too much Christmas shopping, but we borrowed a wheelchair that had been my mother's and what shopping she did that Christmas she did from that wheelchair with one or the other of us pushing her along. We were saddened in our souls that it had come to that but so thankful to have the chair and her willingness to sit and ride in it; otherwise, Teresa's world would have been so very limited and at a time and season that she had always loved.

We asked her if she wanted to have the Edwards side of the family at her house for Christmas. She did. Bradley and I were trying to do much of the housework by this time, and I told her that I and Aunt Betty and her sister and cousins would do all of the cooking. That seemed to please her. She was so drained and had very few days or even hours of feeling good. She needed things to look forward to. It broke my heart when she asked me during that Christmas, "Do you think I'll make another Christmas, Ma?"

I really didn't know that Teresa had been thinking seriously about her chances of dying (I know I should have) and I can still recall at this moment the jolt that I felt. My response was, "Of course you will," even as I knew that we needed a miracle for it to happen.

After Christmas, in the new year 2000, Teresa wanted to work for her friends John and Trish at their tax office. Part-time was all she could manage, and she worked with a myriad of symptoms. As I look back, I know it was good for her to have that much contact with the outside world, but I marvel that she did it for as long as she did. By the early spring she and Zack had had to move in with us because she could do nothing to maintain her house. Occasionally she would ride out to their place for a day or a few hours. Bradley came over many evenings and every weekend. He kept up their place and worked and worried about Teresa. Almost everywhere she went we pushed her in the wheelchair. Still, she tried to put on a brave face, even to the doctors. I knew we had to have help and I faxed over to Dr. Beard a precise list of symptoms before one of her appointments. This was the pivotal point in moving her toward the crucial decision that would change the rest of her life.

All that spring Teresa suffered terribly, and particularly at night. She coughed a dry cough almost continually. She was extremely fatigued, dizzy and off-balance. She felt that she was breathing through a straw (a coffee-stirrer straw, she would say). Her stomach felt big, like something pushing up on it, and she often gagged after meals or after brushing her teeth and actually threw up many times. She could eat very little real food. She was irritable and depressed and she cracked her knuckles constantly because she felt like she was getting no circulation in her hands and fingers and arms. Her lips sometimes felt tingly. She couldn't sleep even with an anti-anxiety drug because of her breathlessness, her coughing, and an aching in her muscles and joints. Her upper shoulders and chest and occasionally her face broke out with sores and bordered on infection. She craved milk and crushed ice. She also felt like she had the symptoms of sinusitis or influenza most of the time. Teresa took about seven prescription drugs every day including her heart failure regimen, the anticoagulant, the colitis medicine, and the anti-anxiety drug. She occasionally took antibiotics or antihistamines for what seemed to be respiratory infections, and she had several over-the-counter drugs as well. In the middle of the night she would often say she wanted to "punch something" and there was a raging restlessness coursing through her sweet spirit that was difficult to watch. We who loved her tried to define it and understand it and gentle it. I'm not sure we succeeded too well, but I know that God used even that.

To say that I did not feel my own life ebbing away through the big gaping hole in my spirit would be a great dark lie. I did not know how I could endure the dark space that would be left in my life - in all of our lives - if God took the light that was "Ree" away from us. I began to believe, though, that God was trying to prepare us to give her up. I would talk to God and to myself about it. I knew that Teresa would go straight to Him. How could I not want her to be free from suffering? Yet there was in me and I believe in her something that God had put there, something I mentioned earlier, a will to live, a command as Dylan Thomas expressed it to "not go gentle into that good night...rage, rage against the dying of the light." It continued to propel us forward each hour, each day, each agonizing night at a time.

Chapter 7 Transplant Advised

The ejection fraction in Teresa's heart was around 19 or 20 by this time. Patients have gone lower than that and survived. She was so symptomatic and her heart rhythm was so erratic, however, that Dr. Beard thought it was time to talk seriously about a heart transplant. There were a number of fine facilities that performed them, but only one in South Carolina. We went to visit Duke, and while the facility and their success rate were impressive, it did not seem like a match for us. The doctors were brilliant but Teresa did not seem to connect with them on that plane of trust and understanding and compassion she was seeking. We considered a visit to Emory or another of the bigger out-of-state hospitals with sound reputations, but somehow we felt led to MUSC in Charleston. It was about two hours away. I had researched it on the Internet and found their statistics good. Our support system (church, friends, and family) would be closer; follow-up care would be more accessible; and my brother and sister-in-law Henry and Brenda were eager to hand over to us the key to a second home they had recently bought on James Island (twelve minutes from MUSC) for as long as we needed it. Several glitches along the way threatened to thwart the process, but God continued to do miracles with Teresa's insurance coverage and through various dear people who loved us, and Charleston remained our destination.

Dr. Beard got Teresa an appointment on Thursday, May 11, 2000 at 10:00 AM to visit MUSC. There was to be one fairly indicative medical test (a MUGA scan of Teresa's heart), and a consultation with the (head of transplant) cardiologist, Dr. Van Bakel. Terry, Bradley, and I all took leave from work to go with her. We understood this to be an appointment to see if a heart transplant could be an option to save her life and the quality of her life.

Dr. Van Bakel explained what qualifies a patient for transplant consideration: poor prognosis (unlikely to be alive in a year or so) because of heart disease but also having a history of few other health problems (which would help ensure that the transplant would succeed). He said the patient needed a good support system, and he looked around at the four of us and agreed that she would have that. He described a little of what the surgery was like as well as the follow-up care. The actual operation would usually last about six hours, and there would be a hospital stay of ten days to two weeks. The doctor did believe Teresa to be at end stage, but further tests, requiring three-four days, would be necessary, to include testing the pressures inside the heart, a treadmill test, pulmonary tests, X-rays, CT scans, and lab findings. There would be appointments with a financial counselor, a social worker, and a psychologist. If the patient qualified, he/she could expect a wait of six to eight months for a donor organ to become available. The patient would need to remain in the Charleston area for two months after being released from the hospital for physical therapy, biopsies, and other monitoring for rejection and infection, the two big threats. There would be a long list of drugs. We left feeling overwhelmed but we knew that this was the right course of action. Teresa was, of course, apprehensive, but we told her she had forgotten what it was like to feel good, and that she had to grab this chance at life. We were to await a call concerning scheduling of the "work-up," as it is called in the transplant process.

By this time Teresa had begun to noticeably swell with the fluid she was retaining because of her heart's poor performance. This fluid had been in her lungs to some degree for a while, causing her coughing and shortness of breath. Her ankles were next to show evidence of it, then her stomach and her calves and thighs. Dr. Beard managed her care when she came back to Columbia between the Charleston visits, and he was able to keep her out of the hospital with 200 mg. of Lasix per day and occasionally some Zaroxolyn, which is a more powerful diuretic. She continued to be monitored for her anticoagulation factor, which one time soared to 8 on the scale, prompting her to be advised to do nothing with any sharp object, not to perform any chores, only to reduce her Coumadin and rest until the reading could be taken again with, hopefully, better results. I think of all the things that could have happened to Teresa and didn't: the slightest injury or fall while her bleeding risk (measured by what is called the I.N.R) was so high could have been devastating; another stroke when the I.N.R. was low could have eliminated her chances for transplant or ended her life immediately; her iron, potassium, glucose, etc. could have gotten dangerously low or high; and any number of other factors could have complicated the process or threatened her life at this time.

After the appointment in May with Dr. Van Bakel, we came home to await the scheduling of the three-day workup. We felt that things were really beginning to happen now, and a sense of anticipation along with a sense of relief and dread and joy and fear mixed all together descended upon us. The greatest fear I began to have was that they might find something in the workup that could prohibit transplant. What if her ulcerative colitis was too severe? What if her lungs were too weakened? What if they thought her finances would not support the cost of the operation and follow-up? What if they thought she was too discouraged mentally to manage the ordeal of this? What if and what if and what if? But God is not a God of "What if's?" and He was teaching us that bit by bit. He showed us each step to take. If there was one we couldn't manage to take, He prodded us on to someone He found that was willing to be used by Him.

Dr. Van Bakel told us on May 11 that the work-up would be scheduled for a couple of weeks after that initial appointment. We waited for a call but two weeks passed and it did not come. We called back to Charleston and spoke with the scheduler. She said there was some difficulty getting all of the appointments that Teresa needed scheduled into a three-day period, especially since summertime was approaching and people who needed to see her there were taking vacations, etc. That seemed reasonable to us, I suppose, but meanwhile, Teresa continued to swell and have her breathing difficulties and all of her other symptoms. After another week or so, I decided to e-mail Dr. Van Bakel. I was apologetic and told him we were new to this and did not know how things were supposed to work, but Teresa's workup had not been finalized, and if he could tell us something to reassure us, that would be wonderful. The next day someone called and gave us a date to be in Charleston.

I was out of school by this time and was thankful for the hours I could spend with Teresa. Some days we watched a lot of television. I tried to find things that she could eat. Occasionally we would get out the wheelchair and go somewhere. Friends from church visited her. She liked to sit out on our back patio if it was cool enough. We had a big window fan that we set on a chair to blow directly into her face. Terry was overwhelmed at how sick she had become. He could not sit and just watch her, so he began a project that was therapy for both of them. For as long as I can remember they had loved flowers and gardening. They both loved the sound of running water. (The screensaver on our computer was the aquarium one!) Teresa had had a fish tank in her room for a long time during high school and college. Terry began to build, in our backyard, a real little fish pond with all sorts of plans for flowers and fishes. We were encouraged and helped by our friends Penny and Ronny who already had undertaken and completed a similar pond in their yard. It was something Terry could do and something Teresa could watch him do when she was able to go outside. It kept her mind occupied a bit from other worries, as she enjoyed being with her dad and watching the dragonflies, butterflies, songbirds, and hummingbirds that seemed to be cheering the project ahead.

A heart cath was part of the workup that Teresa would have in Charleston. In order for them to do the cath, she would have to come off of her anticoagulant several days ahead of time to decrease the danger of bleeding during the procedure. This always made all of us nervous. While too much Coumadin was not a good thing, none or too little increased her chances of a stroke. Dr. Beard, our cardiologist in Columbia, had said once, "Nothing is more devastating than a stroke." I recalled the night she had had the stroke in 1996 and all of the things that had rushed through my mind. I remembered realizing in that moment and that situation that only God could fix it. And He had. Dr. Beard kept Teresa's I.N.R. as near as possible to the desired range. When it fluctuated, we did exactly what we were told to get it back to the right level. We were always nervous, though, when she had to come off of the anticoagulant for some reason: dental work, the defibrillator, and other procedures such as this cath coming up in June.

I don't know what we ever did to deserve the love and support we began to feel from so many people, but I'm sure we could not have made it if God had not put these folks into our lives during the wait for that workup and subsequently the transplant. We felt the prayers and we saw tangible acts of love that we had never anticipated. O.B. Baker, Terry's longtime good friend and shop owner where he worked, decided to have a fundraiser for Teresa during June. A group of men in his and Terry's lodge gave themselves to this effort.

Terry had said, "O.B., we don't even know yet if they're going to take Teresa as a transplant candidate. That's what the workup will tell us."

O.B responded, "Oh, yes, they **are**! They're going to take her. Teresa is going to get this second chance and I mean to help her get there." O.B. and his wife Rebecca had given Teresa a playpen when she was born. We kept that playpen for years in our attic even after the girls outgrew it. As I look back now, I see that little playpen as a sort of stage on which Teresa first began to play out her life as a tiny child. O.B.'s love and efforts that summer of 2000 helped to give her another stage for the new life she was hoping to have if she got her new heart. The money was certainly needed and appreciated, but the love and the friendship behind the fundraiser overwhelmed us in a way that is, even now, hard to express.

Chapter 8 Evaluation Underway

We went to MUSC on July 10 to begin Teresa's evaluation, which would determine her suitability for transplant. We had been told it was an exhausting study, but necessary for knowing with certainty that this was the right choice medically, physically, emotionally - from the MUSC medical professionals' standpoint and from ours. Teresa had twenty plus vials of blood drawn. Other diagnostic tests included pulmonary tests, scans, EKGs, echo ultrasounds, a stress test and kidney function tests. These were for determining health factors beyond what the blood results would show them.

We met with a dietician, a very bright woman who told Teresa exactly what she needed to eat while waiting for her heart. Her protein level had dropped to 12.5. It needed to be close to 20 or 21 at the time of transplant. The nutritionist told Teresa that in order to optimize herself for transplant she needed to limit her salt, eat no processed meat but instead to have fresh chicken, beef, pork, unsalted nuts, and to drink three of the canned nutrition drinks a day. At this point she did not need to limit fat or sugar. I wondered how we would accomplish this with Teresa's current eating habits, and it did turn out to be a battle, but the results were good.

We met with a social worker who presented to us all of the struggles that a transplant patient's recovery entailed, medically and emotionally and financially. We learned that some patients take thirty-five different medicines. The financial burden is great. The biopsies are ongoing. The fear of rejection and infection are constant. Sometimes there is a weight or swelling problem. The steroids would cause mood swings. These were things Teresa had to know to make a decision, but it was hard to face the negative aspects of it all. We knew we must concentrate on the positives, and there were so many of those presented to us during those three days too.

A nurse transplant coordinator met with us. These are vital people to the recovery process, and they were trained magnificently to do their jobs. Diane York had been with MUSC for more than ten years. She told us more about the anti-rejection drugs which would suppress the immune system to prevent the body's rejection of the transplanted organ, the biopsies to detect rejection after transplant, and the need to guard against infections with various immunizations. She told Teresa that after her work-up, all of the information learned about her case would be presented in a committee meeting of the professionals there and they would determine if she would be a candidate and contact her. She would be placed on the list if she wanted to pursue the transplant. When she received a call about a donor organ being available, she could refuse it at that time if she felt she wasn't ready. However, after two refusals, a patient is taken off the list until a firmer decision about being a recipient could be made.

Other appointments we had included a financial counselor who took Teresa's insurance information and told us of projected costs for surgery and follow-up; a psychiatrist, who asked some questions of her and us and prescribed some Ativan to help her sleep at night; and a pulmonary doctor who told Teresa that her very big heart was taking up lots of space in her chest and that, while her lung function tests were not normal, he believed that to be because of her heart problems and he did not foresee that her lungs would prevent transplantation.

Amidst all of this I had a moment of epiphany that helped me realize one great reason why parents feel the burden they do when a child, even a grown one, is seriously sick. The psychiatrist asked Teresa what her childhood had been like. Sometimes, like Terry, Teresa would wait a moment or sometimes several moments before answering a question. She was feeling so down, physically and emotionally, during these last months, and she had almost always spoken softly when conversing with others anyway. (Dr. Beard told someone that when Teresa spoke her wedding vows, that was the loudest he had ever heard her talk!) After Dr. Hunt's question, she got this faraway look in her eyes, and when she looked back to him, she quietly but firmly responded, "It was wonnnnnderful," drawing out the first syllable for emphasis. I was pierced to the core of my soul. While I certainly knew then and know now that we were not perfect parents or a perfect family, I also knew that Teresa had considered her childhood smooth and joyful and trouble-free. I was glad for that. The painful realization that there was nothing we could do to fix this for her now, to restore "wonnnnnderful" to her, was what wounded me so. God uses such wounds to His glory, however, and He was to show me even that.

Dr. Jack Crumbley, the doctor who would actually perform the transplant surgery, was the last appointment in the three-day workup. What an upbeat guy we found him to be. Accompanying the sparkle in his eye was a terrific sense of humor, and behind that there was a quiet confidence and a matter-of-factness about what he did that immediately soothed our chafed psyches. We could almost pretend this was gallbladder surgery or an appendectomy if we had not heard all of the other details. He asked Teresa some questions about her symptoms. He said, "I think we need to get busy," meaning, we knew, that he would do his part to improve things for her. A few months after surgery he expected she would be able to resume many of the usual activities healthy people pursue.

Dr. Crumbley told us he had been at MUSC since the heart transplant program started. He asked Teresa if she wanted children, to which she replied, "Yes, whether I have one or adopt one, I do want children." He told her that in three to four years she may possibly consider a pregnancy, that there were a few post-transplant heart patients out there who had carried a pregnancy to term. He gave her every reason to have hope.

We left Charleston with much to contemplate. Definitely Teresa wanted this chance at life, but the recovery would not be easy nor the future certain. The deciding committee of professionals met each Thursday to discuss prospects for patients who have been evaluated for transplant. They have the clinical data and the opinions of each person there. We were told that they would contact Teresa about whether and when she would go on the list. One of the nurses in clinic told us that the list was quite short at MUSC at that time. We knew, though, that the wait could still be months at best.

Chapter 9 The Life-Changing Call

We returned home and resumed life as we had come to know it. Work on the little backyard pond continued. We kept in close contact with Dr. Beard's office. I bought protein drinks and Teresa drank as many of them as she could. Folks visited. And prayed. And cried. And did so many things to show that they cared about her and us. Teresa continued to feel wretched and I know she was dreading the ordeal ahead. I reminded her again that she had forgotten what it was like to feel good. She needed to form a vision of herself after transplant, well and strong and able to do so many of the things she had had to give up.

The transplant coordinator called on July 7 to say that MUSC was accepting Teresa as a candidate for transplant. It was a Friday. She said the list in Charleston was very short and that there was a possibility she might even get a heart over the weekend. Did Teresa want to wait and be listed on Monday, July 10? Teresa said, "Yes," that she did want the weekend to try to get herself together and fully prepared. So on Monday, July 10, she was officially listed. We packed a bag for each of us. We made a list of people to be called. Our friend Penny had all house keys and plans to feed our pets and care for the fish pond. My school principal knew that Teresa had been listed and even though school was to start in less than a month, she knew I may not get to begin the year if Teresa got a call for the heart before that time. I talked with the coordinator of medical leave at my school district's office and she helped me get the paperwork in order for family medical leave. I had my brother's house keys and all insurance documents ready.

The first days after Teresa made the list, we were jumpy every time the phone rang. MUSC had all of our numbers. We kept a phone with us at all times. Teresa was to receive a beeper or pager in a couple of weeks so that she could be reached through it at any hour. In the meantime we had all phone lines as accessible as we could make them. Teresa called the transplant coordinator with some questions from time to time: Will I need blood? Can my family give? Please tell me again what my blood type is. Can we donate my old heart for research - maybe to MUSC or NIH, where I was treated earlier in the disease? How long will we have to get there when I get the call? They were patient to answer each question she had. As the days went by, we calmed down some. We decided to accept the fact that things most likely wouldn't happen so quickly. We tried to remember that God had a timetable that would be just right. Ecclesiastes 3:1b (NKJV) tells us, after all, that there is a "time for every purpose under heaven." When Teresa felt that she just couldn't make it, we often did, too. We all had heart trouble. But we knew beyond all doubt that we had done every single thing possible. The rest was up to God.

It was two weeks after Teresa was listed for transplant, on July 23, 2000, that we received the call at about 11:00 PM. There had been an awful storm and our power was out. The first call did not connect, and then we found that Bradley, who had gone to their house, had just gotten a number on his caller ID of an attempted call. Terry called the number back and got the transplant coordinator who said, "We have a heart for Teresa." It is difficult to describe our feelings and our actions then.

Teresa began, "I can't do this, Mama. I can't. I can't. No! I just can't. Maybe I'm not as sick as we think."

Even as I trembled with fear, I responded, "Oh, yes, Ree. You can do this. You can. It's what we've waited for. We **can** do this. We will. We are."

We began to gather those things we had packed and those we hadn't. The electricity came back on. We called our friend Penny, who called our pastor. Rich came over immediately to have prayer with us. We called my sister Fay and our brothers. Terry called his co-workers Gene and O.B. and our faithful neighbor Mildred. Penny and Ronny came to our house. Bradley's parents Drayton and Nella came. Penny took charge of things I couldn't remember and helped to get us on our way.

The weather was dreadful. It rained torrents and the sky rumbled and crashed. Teresa sat in the front seat and Bradley and I in the back. Teresa constantly admonished Terry not to drive fast. He was afraid we were behind schedule so he drove our Toyota chariot as fast as conditions would allow, maybe faster! At one point we ran over a large plastic pail that was in the road. It made a horrid scraping noise when it lodged under the front of the car and we had to stop for Terry to pry it loose. We made some phone calls along the way. Teresa talked with her friend Sundai and with Tony Sharpe who had recently served as youth minister at our church. Everyone encouraged her and expressed their joy that she was getting this second chance at a quality life. What a ride into, literally, only God knew what!

Chapter 10 Scary Days and Nights

"For He shall give his angels charge over thee, to keep thee in all thy ways. They shall bear thee up in their hands..." Psalm 91: 11 – 12a (KJV)

Here among the rhythms and the rates,
Amidst the precious dates
with life and death...
the angels move.
And as they move,
The flutter of their wings
in splendid cadence
guides the pulse of life...

The following pages are compiled from entries in a journal I began to keep in the first days of Teresa's transplant surgery. There is no need to specifically point to the miracles in this part of her story. You can readily pick them out. God is surely a supernatural God. He proved himself over and over to be bigger than any circumstance that occurred to terrify us and threaten Teresa's recovery. His hand was everywhere. As I read this diary these many years later, I can see God's direction and protection even more clearly now. I also see how much He has let the medical profession learn about various procedures and treatment options since these days. He continues to directly and indirectly heal.

July 24 (Monday)

We arrived at MUSC around 1:30 A.M. A chaplain waiting outside took us to the ninth floor. Our friends Jerry, Gail, and Joey Rogers were vacationing in Charleston and getting ready for a family wedding. They had arrived before us and were waiting there. Melinda had driven from Columbia with her friend Nick and they, too, were waiting. I remember that wheelchair making its final turn toward Teresa's destination and Melinda running to meet Teresa. Teresa said, "I don't know if I can do it, Lin." Melinda hugged her sister and reassured her. There was a high sense of excitement and foreboding as well. The chaplain had us stand beside Teresa and he prayed before leaving.

The staff on ninth floor were wonderful. They drew the necessary blood, asked all the questions, and did the chest X-ray. Teresa took a shower in antiseptic soap and shampooed her hair and Terry, always her hairstylist, dried it. By this time, we had precious friends and family around us in a sacred circle: besides Melinda, Nick, Gail, Jerry, and Joey, Bradley's parents and his brother had arrived, as well as Bobby and Becky Scott, Penny Thomas, and Chris Bradley. Homer and Betty (Terry's brother and wife) were there with their son J.K. and his wife. There was a powerful spirit of support in that big hospital room and a powerful sense of God's presence in every corner. I don't think the staff could quite believe what they were seeing. The nurses on 9W were kind and compassionate, reassuring Teresa continually. Dr. Pereira talked to her and enrolled her in a study being done with a new anti-rejection therapy. We saw that Doctors Crumbley and Van Bakel were in conference at the nurse's station.

Mike, one of Terry's customers from Columbia, happened to be a patient in the hospital that night. Mike had had three transplant surgeries, a heart the first time, and two years later another heart along with a kidney. He was being treated for a problem with infection and was getting better - walking the corridors of the ninth floor. He came into Teresa's room to encourage her. He wore a mask to guard against hospital germs, but he seemed well and had a great spirit; he made a speech of sorts standing there in her room that amazed us and all of our supporters. This was another evidence of God among us.

We thought the surgery might begin at 3:30 A.M. but the donor heart had not arrived. Then we thought 6:00, then 8:30. We aren't sure about what caused the delay, unless the donor heart was flying and the weather **was** very bad so that could have held things up. We understood that one surgeon harvested the organ and the other one waits at the recipient's end preparing for surgery. Dr. Crumbley and Dr. Van Bakel came into Teresa's room early in the morning. We did not know what to expect. They had told us early in our visits to MUSC that if it was determined that the donor heart was not a good enough match or was not in good shape after harvesting that the surgery would be canceled and the recipient would have to return home to wait again. But everything was a "go." Dr. Crumbley asked Teresa if she had any further questions.

She replied, "I just want to go to sleep."

With his quick sense of humor, he retorted. "What did you do last night? Why didn't you sleep then?" She smiled her best smile.

They took our Ree to pre-op holding about 10:00. Bradley, Terry, and I went along. Before 10:30 we said good-bye and she was wheeled out. Her last words before leaving were, "Tell them all that I love them." What we felt after they wheeled her away was a sense of unreality mixed with an acute shock of reality at the same time. What we knew must happen to return Teresa to a normal life was underway, with all of its wonder and magic and all of its risks combined. The wait began. It was truly a time to trust God for miracles and a time to say thank you to Him for this chance for Teresa to be reborn, really, in a physical sense. There were a great number of people pleading with Him for her life in those hours and in the days and weeks afterward. Some of these people we had never met, but they had heard Teresa's story through a friend or family member or in the workplace or at their church. We can never say thank you enough.

Our family and friends of the night before waited with us throughout the long hours of surgery. Rich and Larry, our pastor and associate pastor, and Patty and Pam, two dear friends of mine from school, also came to wait. We visited, met some other patients' families, and watched the clock. They had said the transplant would take about six hours. At 4:30 we got the word that they were warming her up. We assumed this meant that she was coming off of by-pass and the surgery was concluding. We expected to hear at any time that she was at least in ICU. Everyone waiting was so relieved - and so exhausted, especially all of those who had come from Lexington and Columbia late the night before. We hugged all of them and sent them back home with promises to stay in close touch as Teresa progressed. Homer and Betty stayed. Bradley's brother, Martin, also stayed. While Teresa was receiving her new heart, Bradley's grandmother was dying of cancer. She passed during the afternoon while Teresa was still in surgery, so Bradley's parents, Drayton and Nella, had to return to Lexington. They spent many hours over the next several days going up and down the highway. One life in their family was taken and one was given back that day.

The hours wore on after everyone left. We began to worry as 4:30 turned into 5:30, then 6:30, then 8:00. The transplant nurse called once during those hours, but she was fairly noncommittal, just reporting that they were watching Teresa in these crucial hours immediately after surgery. We were nearly frantic when we looked up to see Dr. Crumbley striding down the hall toward us somewhere around eight o'clock. We could tell from the look on his face that all was not well. He seemed haggard and "shell-shocked." His face was flushed. There was no hint of the twinkling humor we had seen in him on other occasions. His first words were, "Where is her husband?" Bradley had lain down on a sofa in an adjoining waiting room. His brother woke him and steered him down the corridor to where we stood with the surgeon. Bradley was so exhausted that he was veering from side to side of the little hallway, fighting his way back from sleep. Dr. Crumbley's words to us were, "She has bled. We don't know why. We went back in to see if we could see why. She has bled from every place we opened. It has subsided some, but she is still bleeding. She's receiving blood products - plasma and platelets - but she's not out of danger. We'll see how she does overnight." This was a dark moment for us - fatigued yet so very hopeful throughout the day, we were reduced to tears of discouragement. All we could do was wait upon the Lord and wait for morning. Homer and Betty needed to go home, but never even considered it after Dr. Crumbley's report. We thought we would lose Teresa that night.

Bradley, Terry, and I did get to see her in ICU late in the evening for a moment. The nurse on 9 West had tried to prepare us for what it would be like afterwards. She had told us that in the ICU there would be a ratio of one nurse to one or maybe two patients. The patient would be swollen from the bypass and from the massive initial dosage of prednisone and there would be IV's, respirators, and various other lines and tubes hooked up for drainage, monitoring, for use in case of emergencies, etc. When we got in to see Teresa, there were two nurses working with her, administering the blood products that were racing against her loss of blood. She was, of course, unconscious, pale as moonlight, and so very swollen. Her head looked to be the size of a basketball and about that round. I thought of how very little immune system she now had. I was afraid to get very close. We were so numb. The only words we could manage to speak were the words, "We love you, Ree. Rest. You're on the way." I couldn't help but wonder if this would be the last time we would see her in this life, if she was on her way to the Father even as we stood in the room. We had no inkling of what was yet to happen during this night.

July 25 (Tuesday)

The ICU unit was on the third floor in a part of the hospital that was undergoing construction. There was no waiting room nearby. We were sent to the 10th floor ICU waiting room (which had recliners along both walls for the family members of seriously ill patients who were in the hospital to sleep) for the night. Homer stayed around in our prior waiting room to answer the phone if it rang. Bradley and Terry found two empty recliners across the room from Betty and me. The lights were out and people were trying to grab a few fitful hours of sleep all around us. Not having slept for more than forty hours, we pulled our jackets and blankets up, prayed some more prayers, and closed our eyes. In the middle of the night, the hospital fire alarm went off. We knew there had been storms in the area, but at first we were not unduly alarmed, thinking perhaps the alarm had been pulled by accident. But it continued to sound and hospital personnel closed the doors along the hall. This would not be the last time we would hear this sound during Teresa's stay at the hospital - the clanging sound of a block of rooms or a section of the hospital being closed off against the danger of fire. What a chill it sent through me. And what of Teresa, I thought, fighting for her life on another floor of this hospital? I looked out to see a light flashing (not blue or red but clear) and men running along the top of the building next door. I began to contemplate several possible scenarios, but tried to remain calm. In my sleep-deprived state, I thought maybe I was dreaming. We were not contacted that Teresa was not holding her own in ICU, and I kept telling myself that was good news. I wanted to trust the two nurses who were working with her when we left her the night before. And I prayed some more. I'm not sure when the alarm finally quit sounding.

First thing early Tuesday morning Terry, Bradley, and I went toward ICU to visit Teresa. When we peered through the windows of the ICU, what we found was an empty, dark unit, a hospital ghost town of sorts. The ICU had been vacated . We saw no patients, no doctors, nurses or other staff, no light, no activity. We knew then that something had gone terribly awry in the hospital during the night. Someone (medical staff) saw our obvious bewilderment, approached us, led us to another area, and summoned the nurse supervisor for this area. It was then that we were told that the power had gone out in the night due to a transformer blowing. The backup generator had not worked and all of the ICU patients had been moved to the recovery room area. We were led through a "war zone" of patients, many of whom appeared not to be long for this world. It was devastating to see. A tiny child was the first to catch our attention - a small girl no more than two years old, sleeping peacefully but being constantly monitored with an array of equipment. Another was a gentleman who appeared to be hooked up to some type of life support or heart/lung device. Then there was an older child or young teenager who had apparently been in a life-altering accident. Another appeared to be in something like a Stryker frame. We were led through a large room of such patients to a small, separate back room which we were told was very near the operating rooms. Since Teresa was immuno-suppressed, this was an isolation room of sorts, I suppose. This was where we would visit her during this day.

I was paralyzed with the news of her bleeding the night before. I guess this paralysis was the reason I had not fallen apart at that time at the sight of her. On this day, though, I nearly did. Her head and body were unbelievably swollen. Her head was still the size of a basketball. Her eyes were open but they were merely slits. Tears were sliding from the corners of her eyes. She glanced at us sideways. We told her we loved her. She was still bleeding, we were told. Today I seemed to see every single tube - they were everywhere. There was a big line in her neck, the ventilator tube and something else in her mouth, and all of the monitor wires and IV lines for medicine.

There were still two nurses working with her. They were administering blood products and monitoring very closely her vital signs. We did not stay long because we could tell it was intense work. They did not appear to be able to talk to us very much but reassured us as much as they felt they could. Teresa did not look like someone who was doing well. As fast as they could move the blood products into her, they were.

As we visited throughout the day things seemed to improve slightly but the pressure in her lungs was high and they seemed concerned about that. They began to talk of returning the patients to the ICU area as soon as it could be determined that the power would stay on.

Teresa's nurse said, "I hope they don't move them too soon. I don't think she (Teresa) likes to move."

We encountered Dr. Crumbley once during the day when he and Dr. Van Bakel and the residents made rounds. Terry told him he looked better than he had the night before. He asked how he had looked. I told him. He was glad that Teresa had made it through her first night, but he was still guarded in his prognosis.

The State newspaper in Columbia ran an article on Teresa's transplant on July 25. Her picture was there with the headline "Second Midlands Resident Gets Heart Transplant." A young girl about nine years old had been transplanted ten days before Teresa in the Children's Hospital at MUSC. She had been very near death when she received her heart and many prayers had gone up for her as well. Her path and Teresa's would soon cross during their recovery and further along the journey as well.

Chapter 11 One Step Forward, Then...

July 26 (Wednesday)

They did move the patients back into ICU during Tuesday night. We visited early that Wednesday morning, July 26. Teresa was still on the ventilator but she was mouthing things to us and wanted a pencil and paper so she could try to write. She asked, "How many days did I sleep?"

She did get off the ventilator on this Wednesday morning after being on it for about 36 hours. Her voice was low and raspy after having the ventilator tube. She still had oxygen in a kind of mask over her nose. They thought her bleeding was beginning to subside, but she was still getting blood products.

Sundai came to the hospital and I went with her in the afternoon to see Teresa. Teresa seemed to know her and softly spoke the word "Sundai" when she saw her. Sundai was very encouraging, as she always, always had been, and told Teresa she would see her on Saturday.

They taught Teresa how to hold the heart-shaped pillow and cough. They wanted her, as soon as possible, to blow into the spirometer so that they could keep her lungs clear of fluid.

Terry and I thought things were good enough that we could go to my brother's house and sleep on this Wednesday night instead of sleeping in the 10th floor recliner room. Bradley insisted that he would stay in the recliner room where the ICU family members were.

July 27 (Thursday)

The night nurse in ICU called me in the early hours of the morning (about 2:30) to say that Teresa was asking for her mother. I could not tell whether I should translate this into "Things are not well" or not. Later I would realize that this **was** the correct translation. We left the house and got there about 2:45. They let me stay the rest of the night beside her bed. She wanted me to hold her hand. I think part of the problem was that she had looked down and seen her feet and the swelling had terrified her. Also, I think clinically that her numbers were not good for blood pressure and heart rate, etc. Teresa's nurse was a contract nurse who said she had taken care of cardiac patients but never a transplant. This alarmed me, but I was thankful she had called me and that she allowed me to stay in that room that night.

Teresa was rather fitful during the day. She would sleep a bit and seem to be awake for a while, able to answer softly when we asked her something. The doctors and nurses were beginning to be concerned about her kidneys. The output seemed to be lessening. Lasix did not work and neither did dopamine, but finally they found a combination that seemed to work during the evening. This, I believe, is because I had called Penny again and asked that the prayer chain start for that purpose.

July 28 (Friday)

Teresa had a raging headache in the ICU during the night. She opened her eyes wide and said, "My head is pounding, pounding!" They were giving her something called Tylox, I believe, when she was in pain. The blood pressure figures seemed very high on the monitor to me, as they had all along since the surgery.

Then this morning she was sleeping and she didn't seem to be responding to much. I mentioned this to the nurse and she said Teresa was catching up from the surgery and from not sleeping well at night. Teresa had seemed more responsive earlier in the week than she did today, though. It really worried me.

During this afternoon she had a nightmare. She was sleeping propped up and she opened her eyes wild and wide and began to push herself up out of the bed. We told her not to get up. Her response was "I **have** to get up. I **have** to get up from here. I **have** to, Mama. **I have to. I have to**!" She then tried to rip the oxygen tube from her nose. It took the nurse and me to hold her in the bed. It scared me terribly.

Teresa began telling us that she couldn't see very well. Part of the wall clock seemed to be missing from her vision field when she looked at it. We mentioned this to the doctors and nurses and they said that often the prednisone affected vision after transplant surgery and that this would improve.

July 29 (Saturday)

We had lots of company on Saturday – such an encouragement to us. Paris, the nurse in ICU, washed Teresa's hair with a special shampoo they have for patients who are not yet able to get in the shower. Teresa was so very weak and she still had all of her chest drain tubes.

She felt better after the shampoo and was ready to see some of the folks who came. Some of her church friends and some friends of Terry's and mine even got to go into ICU and speak to Teresa. Melinda was here and she had everyone wash up and wear a mask who went in there. She was carrying out the protocol and doing her part for the warfare on germs.

Teresa continued to tell us again that she could not see as she thought she should. She was still using the clock as an example - half of the clock was in a shadow, she said. I didn't feel good about this, but told myself that this would improve as some of the medicines were reduced.

This was to be the first day that Teresa would remember clearly after her surgery. Although she had been answering our questions fairly coherently since Wednesday, she didn't feel that she was "totally back" until today. I clarify the "coherently" with "fairly" because there was one incident that we particularly found humor in (later!) that occurred during these hazy days. The respiratory therapist had visited Teresa to emphasize how important it was for her to increase her lung capacity and keep those lungs clear. He wanted her blowing in the spirometer as vigorously and often as she could. She was somewhat reluctant. He told her it was so very necessary because they would have to go in and drain her lungs if they became congested. She was all concerned and confused about the swelling she had - everywhere, but especially in her feet. One of those early post-transplant mornings when we went in to visit, she was very sleepily and weakly holding the spirometer as she looked up at us and reported, "That man says I have to blow in this thing. Otherwise, he is going to run something down my mouth to my feet and try to get the fluid out of them." She wouldn't change this story even when we tried to explain that her lungs were the issue. "I **know** what he said," she kept repeating. "I **know** what he said..." She didn't remember a bit of this when we told her about it much later.

July 30 (Sunday)

Teresa was hoping to get into a regular room. They wanted her blood pressure to come down some before moving her out of ICU. They also wanted to get the chest and neck lines and the pleura-vacs, which empty fluid from the lung cavities, out before the move, and hers were still necessary. She was able to take small steps inside her ICU room with a great deal of help in maneuvering both her and the array of equipment and lines connected to her. Teresa was still swollen, but not as much as in the early hours after surgery. Were we getting used to things this way? Were we relaxing at all? Maybe just the tiniest bit - we were so thankful to have made it through the bleeding episode and the terrible headache. We knew that anything could happen yet, though, so we would be reserved in our optimism for the next several days and weeks.

July 31 (Monday)

July 31 is my sister's birthday. Fay was taking care of our mother in Saluda, where both Terry and I had grown up. Mama was a total invalid with Alzheimer's disease by now. Fay had not missed a day of calling to check on Teresa. She passed our prayer requests on to the churches there in Saluda and many of those folks were calling Teresa's name to God too. Judy Coleman, a friend of our family for many years there who had had heart problems herself since she was a young woman, stayed in touch with us all throughout Teresa's struggles. The local paper gave updates on Teresa's progress regularly and cards arrived with encouragement, promises to continue to pray for her, and descriptions of how they were inspired by her courage and by what God was doing in her healing.

The staff took the big intravenous lines out of Teresa's neck and chest on this day, the 31st. They replaced the A-line from the left side with another line on the right. She felt that she was gradually being liberated but it was slow progress. While they wanted to get her pleura-vacs out before moving her, they decided that she could be monitored on a regular floor and made plans to move her. We were all so excited. The room they would move her to was a filtered room, meaning that the air was not circulated hospital air, but air circulated from outside (fewer germs in it). The same sanitation rules would apply for anyone visiting Teresa during this precarious time in her new room. We made the move rather late in the day, one week after Teresa was transplanted. The room was much larger and really pretty for a hospital room. There was a recliner chair in the corner, so Bradley or I could doze here instead of in a straight chair beside the ICU bed. I was a little nervous about the higher nurse-to-patient ratio but I knew we had to take this step forward to get her well enough to leave the hospital.

Chapter 12 Reaching for Better

August 1 (Tuesday)

Teresa went to physical therapy on August 1. I felt that she was now beginning to see that she could reclaim her health, but she was fearful and anxious and they did not press her to walk so very far or do too much. Her defibrillator had not been removed as they had hoped during her transplant surgery because of the excess bleeding, but they had disconnected the wires. Something about it still being there was on Teresa's mind. I think the shocks she had gotten from it previously were still very vivid in her memory and she knew that those were partly caused by overactivity. She would have to come to fully realize that the device was not necessary for this heart and had no connection to it. This heart pounded fairly hard sometimes, too, and I think she was worried that she would overtax it. She would come to trust her physical therapist, Lana, before the physical therapy ended, but day one was a little soon for her.

August 2 (Wednesday)

She did do better in physical therapy on August 2. She walked twice as far as the day before. It was a nerve-wracking day, though, because bad news seemed to be abounding. They were concerned about a rash on Teresa's face. They ran tests so that they could rule out Lupus and a dermatologist was to be called in to let us know what to do.

The ophthalmologist came to check Teresa's vision because she persisted in telling all of us that she could not see very well. She had progressed from not being able to see half of the clock to seeing a shadow over half of it to seeing what she described as a "blur" over half of the clock face when she looked at it head-on. They were taking extreme caution with her and while everyone thought that it was just the anti-rejection medication given in such high doses at first, they wanted to be sure. The ophthalmologist's news was not good. After examining Teresa right there in her hospital room the doctor told us that the problem was not in Teresa's eyes but in the vision center of her brain - probably a clot or a bleed, some lack of oxygen at some point along the way since the transplant began. They were going to ask for a CT scan to see what was happening.

Janice and William Harman came from home to see Teresa and to take me out to lunch. Bradley was going to stay with Teresa so I felt comfortable leaving the hospital for a little while. It was great to talk - relaying some of my praises and some of my worries - and eat and relax for a short time. When my friends drove me back to the hospital I insisted they did not have to walk me back in and William drove me to the closest entrance, where I walked up to the elevators and then to Teresa's room. I knew when I entered that something had not gone just right. Bradley, and even Teresa, seemed stunned.

The medical staff had explained earlier in the hospital stay that when the pleura-vacs stopped filling with so much fluid it would be a sign that soon they could be removed, that the drainage from the surgery site would be diminishing. Teresa seemed to have reached this point so they made a decision to take one of the tubes out of her. Bradley said she was fine just after the removal of the tube, but in a short while a flood of drainage began to pour out of her, soaking her gown, her robe, and the bed. Bradley was terrified and angry. He found a nurse for Teresa and then someone else appeared to soothe him through this ordeal. They think the tube had crimped inside of her and the drainage, instead of flowing out, had backed up inside. They did not put the tube back in but they changed the dressing frequently and watched her closely. I could feel how Bradley (and Teresa!) must have felt and I was sorry I had not been there. But God did show Bradley and Teresa that they were stronger than they thought and even this would be resolved.

We had met a family earlier in the hospital stay who also had a family member in ICU with a serious condition. Their grown son had been in an accident that paralyzed his diaphragm, so aside from his other serious injuries they were waiting to see if this paralysis would be permanent or subside as time passed. The young man's mom had been at the hospital and his dad and stepmother as well. They all seemed to get along well. They shared news among themselves as it came through the channels and I remember one day that the dad came into the recliner room and said, "Have y'all seen my wives – either one of them?" This family was clinging together just as ours was. I will never forget what this stepmother said to us in the elevator before our paths diverged, "God wants to know how much you're gonna trust Him." I resolved to never, ever forget those words, no matter how long the journey.

August 3 (Thursday)

Teresa accomplished even more in physical therapy on August 3. She stayed on the treadmill for ten minutes as compared to only two or three minutes before her transplant and this was definitely progress. She also practiced on some steps and on getting up and down from a chair.

As for medical reports on this day: One of the transplant nurses came in and said that Teresa's white blood count had gone up. They were hoping there was not an infection brewing somewhere. The dermatologist prescribed two medicines for her face. They did a CT scan to see what could have happened in Teresa's brain to affect her vision. One of the doctors wanted to order an MRI but Teresa insisted she could not have an MRI with that defibrillator still in her chest. It turns out she was exactly right. Although the leads had been disconnected when her diseased heart was removed, they (or part of them) and the actual metal "box" were still in there and could overheat in an MRI or be affected by the magnetic fields of the procedure. So they did a CT scan instead.

August 4 (Friday)

Teresa slept all night with the help of some Benadryl. They took out the last of the chest tubes on this morning. What a relief! She said she had felt like an animal on a leash must feel. They did have to set up another IV line in her arm from which to draw blood since they were also removing the V-line from her chest. They had a little trouble getting it in but finally did. Her nurses today, Stephanie and Michelle, were wonderful.

As far as medical reports, Dr. Pereira brought the news today that the white blood count was higher still so they began to culture all of her bodily fluids to try to find out what kind of infection so they would know how to treat it. The neurologists also came in. It seemed fairly certain that sometime after surgery Teresa had had two bleeding strokes into the vision part of her brain. Her brain seemed to be compensating, they said, and we knew we would be asking God for yet another miracle to heal her completely of the vision difficulty. She didn't go to physical therapy today. One of the therapists came to her and they walked around the hall. Teresa's friend Kerry came to visit as well as Bradley's relatives Jody, Teresa, Daniel, and Heather.

The MUSC pharmacy told us on that Friday that Teresa's insurance had maxed her $2000 annual limit on drugs. They would only now pay for the immunosuppressants and those would have copays. The bill for the first month looked to be about $600. This could get worse or better. We thanked our dear God and our dear friends for the money that had been raised in the fundraisers so far. We would talk to our MUSC financial counselor on Monday to see if there was some mistake.

August 5 (Saturday)

I stayed with Teresa the night of August 4 so Bradley could try to get some sleep. I felt angry in the night, one of those pity parties maybe. The fire alarm went off between 12:15 and 12:30 and didn't stop until nearly 1:00 AM. It was not just that, of course, but a culmination of stress. I began to replay in my mind the ten-hour wait without hearing much during surgery, the bleeding she experienced after, the failed transformer that night and the failure of the backup generator, the two hemorrhagic strokes, the near-miss with the scheduled MRI, the chest tube flood, and then the medicine bill which we had not been advised about. The fire alarm going off sent me over the edge. There was a fire alarm in the hospital when we came for workup, a justifiable one when the transformer blew on the 24th, a brief alarm another night, and then the one on this night. I felt my own heart pounding, pounding, pounding. How must it affect the patients! I thought maybe God was trying to show me something I was not catching on to. I was discouraged.

Late in the afternoon of August 5, after some company left, Teresa was sitting in the recliner in the hospital room when she looked at me, wild-eyed and panicky, and said, "My heart is beating REALLY fast." I went to her hall monitor and saw the word *Tachycardia* in red and, I think, the number 166. The nurses were already hurrying our way and they ran EKG strips, checked oxygen levels, etc. A doctor was paged and they all tried to reassure her. She was nearly frantic. They thought she might be fighting a sinus infection and planned to start an antibiotic. Other than that, the fast rate they attributed to the new heart getting used to her and her to it, with maybe a little stress/panic mixed in. I planned to stay the night again.

August 6 (Sunday)

As the next day wore on, Teresa seemed to get over some of her panic from yesterday's episode. She walked about five different times, got her tennis shoes on her feet for the first time since surgery, and did her chest exercises and blowing apparatus throughout the day. She had some company in the afternoon. This was her best day yet.

Terry and I went to my brother's house to sleep. Teresa called to say that her antibiotic would not go into the line in her hand – it backed up there and the line would have to be moved. She was dreading it. I told her to call me back and let me know. I prayed. She did call back about an hour later. The new line went in with no problem and once again we agreed that our God is an awesome God in great and small miracles.

Chapter 13 Homeward to James Island

August 7 (Monday)

Teresa had another CT scan of her head on August 7. It showed "bilateral occipital lobe infarcts" which we learned were strokes in the vision center of her brain – both sides. She had hemorrhaged that night in ICU when she had that horrid headache. The strokes left her with two "raindrops" or "teardrops" as she described them, in her vision in both eyes. The doctors said that it would be a matter of time to know if there would be any further improvement. She would be seen at the Storm Eye Institute there at MUSC.

We remember being thankful that the severe vision loss she had at first (when she could not see the clock on the wall at the foot of her bed) was not permanent – it could have been! Teresa was, once again, learning to live with what might be, without further improvement, a new normal for her. While she would later have other, different problems with her eyes, she was able to drive for many, many years, and never mentioned the "tears" in her vision field unless we asked her. They did fade some over time.

The good news from Room 940 today turned out to be that Teresa was going home! Dr. Pereira said she could and she was all smiles. She walked a bit with the physical therapist. She talked with him, with the dietician, the floor nurse, and the nurse transplant coordinator. She had to choose something to wear and we made several trips to the car.

Her medicine was still a big issue. We finally made it out of the pharmacy at $433. This was not before we talked with the financial/insurance person, the financial/pharmacy person, and Eckerd's, as well as the nurse transplant coordinator. Then they did not charge us for two medicines in the bag and we told them, in an effort to be honest in everything, about it. They said those two had been called and cancelled and wanted to take them out of the bag. We had to convince them to call Diane York, one of the transplant coordinators, and talk with her. Sure enough, Teresa was supposed to have those two as well.

Teresa looked very pretty in her dress and sandals, even though her ankles were swollen and she was self-conscious about that. Her nurse Stephanie, a great one, took Teresa out to the front to meet the car. Happy day!

I felt so very thankful to be this far. I did still worry about blood pressure, her eyes, an infection and the upcoming biopsy. I recall feeling, on the way home that "I am not smart enough, clean enough, or wealthy enough to do this." Remembering the advice/wisdom from August 2, "God wants to know how much you're going to trust Him" seemed to help.

Teresa's blood pressure was 157/70.

More thanksgiving: As I referred to going "home" during these days of journal entries I was meaning my brother Henry and sister-in-law Brenda's second home on James Island. They were so very kind and generous with this well-chosen house they had purchased. Henry had paid close attention to detail (safety, landscaping, etc.); Brenda was a superb, elegant yet practical decorator; and they both wanted the house to be comfortable and livable when they picked it out. My family will always feel such thanksgiving for the use of their home as ours during Teresa's recovery and later as well.

August 8 (Tuesday)

Teresa did not seem to feel very well on her first day away from the hospital. She still complained of headache in the back and around her eyes. We thought it was sinus trouble but I know she worried about the brain bleeds. Her blood pressure was 141/73. Her temperature was 99.3. Her eyes were sensitive to light.

She got up early but lay back down. We went to physical therapy at 11:00 but found out we were not expected to be there after all. Since the next day was biopsy day we would not go back to therapy until Thursday. I brought Teresa and Bradley home then went to the grocery store. They just took it easy – Teresa wrote some thank-you notes. She did not eat very well.

She was up and down today, I guess you'd say. They had told us that the medicines she was on, particularly at first, could make you have mood swings along with physical effects. She told Kevin, Bradley's brother, that she was "wonderful" but she told her friend Gayle Harman she was not feeling great and was worried about her eyes. Tonight she said, "I feel behind. And I am afraid my heart is going to race again and that I am never going to breathe right." I thought these were all legitimate fears, in light of her health before transplant and some of the complications since. I also think she was nervous about the biopsy she was facing the next day, the first since transplant.

August 9 (Wednesday)

Biopsy day. Teresa **was** very nervous. She had blood drawn, then we went to Rutledge Tower to wait. They give "conscious sedation" for the biopsy instead of putting the patient totally out. Afterwards, Teresa said she could feel them making her heart jump as they went in to get the tiny bits of heart tissue to test for rejection.

Sylvia Odom, one of the transplant nurses, saw Teresa in recovery. She looked at the drug card (a list of medicines that Teresa was supposed to bring to every visit). Sylvia had last seen Teresa when she was being moved from ICU to the regular room. We told her about the two strokes and the vision issues. We also asked about the results of cultures on the body fluids and she said those came back okay, so she thought the slight temperature was probably related to the suspected sinus infection.

Dr. Van Bakel saw Teresa also. He checked her medicine list too and said he would decide what to change related to transplant drugs He increased her Benadryl to ½ twice a day and 1 at night. He took out a stitch that had been left in. He increased the Lasix to 40 mg. to try to get fluid off. He also increased the potassium dosage.

After this we went to chest X-ray and then the ECHO lab. It was about 2:00 PM when Teresa was finished and we came toward home. We learned that this was the format most clinic visits would take: register at the registration desk, have blood drawn, vital signs taken, etc., then have whatever procedure was scheduled, see the transplant nurse, then see the physician of the day. After any invasive procedure would be a chest X-ray. The ECHO would be necessary early on but not every time after the initial recovery unless there was a suspected problem.

We rested hard in the afternoon. Teresa's blood pressure was low during the evening. A drop – we were hoping this was good.

August 10 (Thursday)

On the morning of the 10th Teresa's blood pressure was up and her temperature began to climb. I was hoping the antibiotic was going to grab the sinus infection before she stopped taking it.

I wrote today's journal entry while she was in physical therapy about 10:00 AM. She walked the halls as least as long as before and stayed on the treadmill for fifteen minutes plus! Her blood pressure did go up – to 178/70 and Lana, the physical therapist, let her stop for a while. Lana decided to call Diane York and see how high they would let her pressure get. Teresa was fearful, as we all were, of another stroke. She said she felt, or imagined she felt, her head burning.

Lana sent Teresa to Rutledge Tower for Diane to be sure she was okay blood pressure-wise. Diane thought so, telling Teresa again that this would be a gradual process with the exercise increase needing to be incremental in order for her to get used to the new heart.

Good news! We found out that the heart rejection from the prior day's biopsy was 0! Dr. Van Bakel just slightly decreased the amount of prednisone she was taking.

Diane did call to say that one blood level indicator came back low. They would slightly increase her Cellcept. I began to realize that this monitoring of meds would be ongoing for the rest of Teresa's life and I was thankful they knew how to do this for the most benefit and least damage.

August 11 (Friday)

Better numbers the next morning – temp 98.8, blood pressure down to 144/57 and heart rate 82. She walked on the treadmill for 21 minutes at physical therapy. She stood and pushed her own wheelchair out of the hospital!

Sundai and Alec came in the evening (6:00 or so) to see her. Sundai **always** cheered Teresa up.

We ate, and then went to Citadel Mall (terrible rain!) for her to walk for 20 more minutes.

August 12 (Saturday)

August 12, 2000 was Teresa's twenty-fifth birthday.

Kevin, Bradley's brother, and friend Chris Pound came to see her in the morning and so did John and Trish Todd. Then Nella and Drayton came in the afternoon and we all took Teresa to eat at the Crab House. She was rather nervous but she made it. She looked beautiful. We promised her a sterling silver medic bracelet for her birthday.

August 13 (Sunday)

Homer, Betty, and Grandma Clara came the next morning and I fixed some lunch for all of us. When they got here Terry and Teresa were walking in the road in front of the house – 18 minutes in the heat she made it.

We rode Grandma to see the ocean during the afternoon. After they left Teresa asked that we take her to the mall to walk for her second 20 minutes. She made it and then she wanted to shop a bit!

After we got home her nose bled some. I hoped it was maybe due, once again, to her sinus trouble. She couldn't seem to get her temperature totally down to normal.

I wrote some notes during the evening and as I did I thought "How will I ever properly thank these treasured friends?"

Chapter 14 A New Friendship and More Progress

August 14 (Monday)

On August 14 our family met little Vanna Dorn and her family, who were also from Lexington. Vanna was the darling little nine-year-old who had been sick much of her life and received a heart transplant 1 1/2 weeks before Teresa. We met her in physical therapy, along with her dad, mom, and tiny baby brother. They were so very nice and we felt, despite the age difference, we had much in common.

Teresa walked for thirty minutes. Lana asked Teresa to state a goal that she wanted to reach and Teresa told her that her goal was to run on Folly Beach. Lana asked me what my goal for my daughter was, my dream. I responded, "I'll have to think about that one. I haven't dared to dream for her for so long. My goal has been to keep her alive!"

Lana replied, "Well, God already answered that prayer. Think of something else." I promised her I would.

We went to the Folly Beach pier and Teresa walked for thirty more minutes later in the day.

August 15 (Tuesday)

Teresa walked at a steeper incline on August 15 for 33 minutes.

Rich, our pastor, sat with me as I waited for Teresa in physical therapy. He let me talk and talk about things that had happened along the way toward transplant, during, and after. He was a good listener and I was so glad to share that time with him.

Later Teresa and Bradley went to Citadel Mall again for her to walk some more.

August 16 (Wednesday)

Teresa had her second biopsy on August 16. She was nervous but not as much as before. They had prescribed a small dose of Ativan for her. We continued to meet patients each time we went to the hospital who were having various experiences: a man waiting for workup for a heart; a woman three years out from transplant; another man on his second transplant, doing great. This latter gentleman's first transplanted heart had developed coronary artery disease in the small vessels, something they did not know about 12 years ago. He got his second transplant two years ago from this day.

Diane York met with us. She said initial labs they got back from the morning's blood draw looked good. Other results would not be back until Friday. Biopsy results would be available later in the day most likely. We talked to Diane about what information to put on Teresa's medic alert bracelet.

Teresa saw Dr. Van Bakel too and he said the blood levels looked pretty good. He told her to increase her Lasix to 40 any day that she needed to in order to keep fluid off. He did not want to take her off of the Norvasc yet because of pulmonary hypertension. He seemed pleased overall. He listened to her chest, examined her liver. The Bilirubin number, which had obviously been elevated, was coming down slowly. He did not make medicine changes pending results of biopsy.

We went to the Market jewelry store and ordered her bracelet.

August 17 (Thursday)

Teresa's biopsy result was a 1a this time. She was worried because it was not a 0 again. We knew we needed to trust that this would be okay. The only thing we could think to do differently was to take the immunosuppressant drugs at **exactly** the same time each day instead of **approximately** the same time.

Teresa and Vanna grew to be crazy about each other. Although fifteen years apart in age, we figured they would be friends forever. We gave Vanna a crystal angel we found and on a card we wrote, "For Vanna, because God has had angels watching over us and because He holds our hearts in His hands."

As I read through my journal entries from these days, I realize that there might appear to be a sameness in some of the details of our days in Charleston. I include them here because they show the routine that we had to establish to get Teresa as well as she could be: regular physical exercise that showed some progress each day, regular blood pressure and heart rate checks at home, regular medicine intake, regularly scheduled labs, tests, and clinic visits... While the frequency of these things would eventually diminish, all of them needed to be a part of the long road. When something unusual came up we just had to deal with it.

Establishing her medicine regimen was a complicated process. Some of them needed to be taken at the same time each day. Some were taken several times a day, some once a day, some only a few days a week. We had to write it down. The drugs would change, decrease, or increase depending on the tests and symptoms of her health. Around this time Teresa was taking nine prescribed drugs, five nutritional supplements, and a couple of digestive health medicines. In all, since some of the drugs prescribed involved multiple pills per dose, she was taking between 40 and 50 pills per day!

August 29 (Tuesday)

We knew Teresa was scheduled for a heart cath on August 29, but we did not know it was the *involved* one. They took her back and in about 45 minutes they called us. We thought it was probably over, but they had just gotten her ready for the procedure. She was to have the biopsy (neck) and the catheter in the groin. This one involved lying flat for four hours afterward, with the right upper leg sandbagged. It was probably good that neither Teresa nor I knew too much about this beforehand. Terry and Bradley were able to wait until it was over but they had to leave then. (They had returned to Lexington by this time to resume working.)

Dr. Van Bakel was pleased with the results of the cath – pressures in the heart and other reports they gleaned from that. He changed Norvasc to Vasotec. We were told to call her blood pressure numbers in to their office in about a week. Too high would be above 105 on the bottom or above 160 on top. He reduced prednisone to 15 mg. per day.

Sylvia Odom also talked to Teresa about living her life as normally as possible when the time came that she could go home to Lexington. Sylvia told her she had not been saved to live fearfully – carefully, yes, but to LIVE. I have never forgotten that conversation.

September 2 (Saturday)

We had asked to receive a copy of the pathology report on Teresa's diseased heart. It arrived in the mail on September 2. It was in very technical terms, but we understood enough of the vocabulary (extensive myocardial fibrosis, hypertrophied, infarction, dilated cardiomyopathy, etc.) that Teresa remarked, "It's probably good that I got rid of that one."

Chapter 15 Thanksgiving to Donor Family

September 3 (Sunday)

Today I felt that I could not wait another day to thank the family of the donor who gave Teresa the heart of their loved one and I wrote a letter. The transplant team had told us that we could write and give the letter to them and they would get this to the family. I did not know how soon would be too soon but I wanted to somehow convey to them my sorrow for their loss but the joy that they had given to us in this gift of life. I see from this letter in my journals that I dated it on September 3. I am not sure when I gave this to our transplant team, but I think shortly after I wrote it. They would give the letter to the donor family when they felt they were ready to receive it. I'm not sure when it was sent to them. This is what my heart told me to write:

Dear Donor Family,

I know that your grief is still fresh, and my heart breaks for you. I think of you often and how you must feel, of how you get through each day. And then I think of what extraordinary folks you must be, for out of your great loss you have given that great gift which has helped to save my twenty-five-year-old daughter's life. How do we say thank you?

Teresa is the older of our two daughters. On the day before her twelfth birthday, she was diagnosed with hypertrophic cardiomyopathy, a thickening and stiffening in the heart muscle. Some people have this disease and live relatively normal lives. Her case appeared advanced and serious even at age twelve. She could no longer dance (she was competitively clogging) and could not engage in any sustained strenuous physical activity. Along with the ineffectiveness of the pumping action of her heart, the rhythms were susceptible to going awry and there was a chance that she could die suddenly. It significantly altered our world. While I surely cannot say that I know how you feel at your loved one's loss, I have experienced an agony during the years *that allows me to **imagine** how you must feel. My arms are, figuratively speaking at least, around you.*

Teresa got used to an adjusted normal lifestyle. She fell in love when she was thirteen years old with the boy she would eventually marry. He began going to doctors with us when he was about sixteen or so. They were in some of the same high school classes together, went to their junior and senior proms together, and graduated together. In 1996 Teresa's heart went into atrial fibrillation. She was shocked back into rhythm five times and she took various antiarrhythmic drugs. Nothing could keep her out of atrial fibrillation and so they began to just try to keep her heart rate down and manage it as best as possible. In 1996 she also had a mild stroke, but she recovered. We feel God has been in all of this - every step.

Teresa was still determined to maintain as much of a normal life as possible. She was fatigued and fairly short of breath much of the time. Her stamina diminished. In 1997 she had a cardiac defibrillator implanted in her chest. Some of her doctors thought her disease was nearing end-stage and the defibrillator could bridge her through until transplantation. They did not know how long it would be. The ICD and a regimen of heart failure drugs gave her 2 1/2 more years during which time she married her friend of nearly ten years and finished her degree at a local technical college. While the ICD was wonderful, it terrified her, too, because, since she was in atrial fibrillation, it shocked her sometimes even when her heart was not in a dangerous arrhythmia (five straight times one night, three times another night.) She continued to work part-time for an attorney and then for an accountant. In late 1999 and early 2000 her health took a marked downturn. She had to stop working in April of this year.

Teresa has always loved Christmas and other holidays. She shopped from a wheelchair this past Christmas. She was dizzy when she was on her feet and she felt most days like she was breathing through a tiny straw. For months she did not sleep more than a few hours at night. She held fluid in her legs, lungs, and stomach and could eat almost nothing. When she did eat she was often sick afterward. Her muscles and joints ached. Her muscles deteriorated. She craved crushed ice and ate ice constantly. She and her husband live fourteen miles from us and during these months, after she would visit us, her dad and I would sometimes cry with the pain and helplessness we felt. We convinced Teresa and her husband to let her move to our house so that she was closer to the doctors and neighbors and so that more people would be available to help take care of her.

In May she began to move toward transplantation and toward her new life with your loved one's heart. On July 23 about 11:00 PM my husband heard the words over the telephone, "We have a heart for Teresa." I'm sure you can identify with the feeling we had, albeit it in different circumstances: this is so real, yet so unreal at the same time.

Oh, sweet friends, it has been about six weeks. My tears as I write this are tears of indescribable joy. I want so much to mix them with your tears of sorrow to somehow have you feel, although you don't know us, some of what you have returned to us with your gift.

Why did Teresa get this horrid heart disease? Why has she suffered when other adolescents and young adults seemed to be enjoying a normal lifestyle? Why was your family member plucked from life in his or her prime season? I believe that some things we won't understand this side of heaven. We have to count on a peace that passes understanding. From Ecclesiastes 3:1 (KJV), "To every thing there is a season, and a time to every purpose under the heaven."

I wrote a little poem one time when Teresa was about fifteen years old and undergoing some tests in the hospital that would tell us more about her heart. It's probably not great poetry, but I have shared it with various friends during their dark days and I wrote it from my heart of hearts at that time.

(I included here my Dancing with Joy poem.)

May the life you have helped return to Teresa be one of your "dances with joy."

Most sincerely,

Teresa's mom (and all of Teresa's family)

I would hear from this letter at a later time when Teresa's donor's mother wrote a letter back that laid bare the mother's heart in her, described what her daughter was like, what had happened to her, and how they arrived at the decision to donate her daughter's organs. She sent a picture to us. These are precious, precious documents to me, and as long as I have a memory and a life, I hold them as some of my family's most valuable possessions.

Chapter 16 Transitioning to Lexington

Our last few weeks in Charleston, early in September, we continued in our regimen of careful eating that had been recommended (low fat, low sugar, fairly low salt, etc.), tried to adhere to the drug schedule, went to doctor's appointments and procedures as they were scheduled, went to the scheduled physical therapy, and tried for some extra exercise on our own.

I remember one day we went to walk on Folly Beach. It was about eight miles from my brother's house and we drove our car there, parked, and walked out to where the sand was wet and flat. We had Teresa's little Chihuahua Zack with us by this time, and we thought it might be fun to take him too. We had his long leash, of course, and he was pretty excited. Teresa's balance was still a little off and it was windy on this particular day. We started out okay, but as the walk progressed, Zack began to run around and around us, and we began to walk crazily into each other while attempting not to step on him. Before we realized it we were tangled up and wound up in the leash like thread on a spool. There was probably not much worthwhile exercise on that walk, but it was good for some deep belly laughs and we surely needed that.

We eagerly anticipated the day that Teresa could return to Lexington. Everything progressed toward that, and on the weekend of September 16-17 they allowed a kind of "trial run" home, cautioning her about adhering to their instructions concerning the drug regimen and other protocol like daily blood pressure and temperature checks and being careful around a crowd because of her reduced immunity. On that Sunday she was able to attend church amongst the many who had prayed her through. She was overwhelmed by her welcome at Oakwood and ecstatic to be there. These words were written by reporter Peter Buttress for Lexington's newspaper, *The Dispatch News* the following week:

> *"When the Rev. Richard Wilson, pastor of the Oakwood Baptist Church, planned a special Sunday morning Christian homecoming service for September 17, he didn't know what a true homecoming it would be for one member of his*

congregation. Teresa Taylor, 25, who received a heart transplant July 24, was allowed to come home for the weekend from Charleston where the surgery was performed.

Accompanied by her husband, Bradley, and her parents, Ruth and Terry Edwards, she sat in the balcony of the church. Soon after the service began, the pastor welcomed guests and then he said, "It would be impossible for us to celebrate homecoming today without also mentioning the homecoming of someone who is with us as a gift. Today, Teresa is in the balcony and we praise God for her being here. Taylor stood up and waved as members of the congregation turned and gave her a standing ovation. Becky Scott, a longtime friend, cried. There weren't many dry eyes in the place..."

The Oakwood church family, headed by our close friend Gail Rogers, were planning a bake sale, yard sale, and silent auction for the following weekend, September 23. This event had been planned for a while, and it was another great blessing that Teresa was told the week after the Oakwood homecoming service that she could return home to Lexington on a more permanent basis.

That Friday, September 22, when Teresa came home, it rained fiercely on the way up Interstate 26. I had Teresa's Chihuahua with me and I recall that he sat on the front seat and watched the windshield wipers as they flew back and forth, his head flying back and forth too as he barked at each threatening (at least to him) swipe. If ever a dog could have laryngitis, Zack qualified. My nerves and his were pretty raw and we were thankful to reach our first stop, the hair salon in West Columbia where Terry worked. Teresa fell into her daddy's arms there and greeted his coworkers who had been such a support to her and all of us. A reporter was there to interview us and I remember saying that the rain had to be the angels crying tears of joy for Teresa being returned to her family and to life.

The event held at our church that homecoming weekend raised about $9,000 for Teresa's medical bills. Along with other fundraisers like the ones O.B. Baker, Bill's Pickin' Parlor, Bradley's cousins and other friends had organized, we felt we had funds to help transition us through those early days of high drug bills, hospital deductibles, travel expenses, and medical supplies. Teresa had been awarded disability benefits after her stroke and Medicare was her primary insurance provider, with Bradley's plan at his father's business secondary. She would be considered disabled for one year after transplant and then reevaluated. We knew many of the costs would be ongoing, but we now had time to get settled in, get her settled in, and we could put the concern about the health insurance plans and choosing exactly the right ones a bit further into the future. We are thankful for the insurance she had had, did have, and as I look back, would yet have throughout an unbelievable medical journey. There would be some trying years ahead with some high deductible coverage, but God provided at every turn, and the fundraisers – this Oakwood one and others – were part of that provision.

The money raised was such a great gift, but as I often say, the friendship behind the monetary help and the "faith in action" concept awed and humbled us in a way that can't be described in words. That countless people, from family, friends, and acquaintances to complete strangers, would reach out in so many ways that would be indelibly carved into our lives still makes me cry. I was quoted in a newspaper article about the church fundraiser as saying, "I think of the people I can name off one after another that have been more precious than gold." I still see clearly in my heart and mind the faces of the saints these many years later and always will.

Maybe in my description of one special friend you will see a representation of the multitude of angels who hovered around us, praying, crying, smiling, laughing, protecting, sustaining, encouraging, cheering, healing, providing. Some of these were in our lives even before Teresa's diagnosis and some joined the journey along the way. Penny is a symbol of a multitude...

Chapter 17 Penny

After a particularly hard day I would sometimes feel like "What next?" Besides telling God that I didn't understand why some of these things were happening, I could tell my friend Penny.

Oh, that everyone had just one penny worth what my Penny is worth. What a wealthy people we would be! "Greater love hath no man than this, that a man lay down his life for his friends." John 15:13 (KJV) Penny gave some of her life away to us every day that Teresa was in Charleston. Actually, it began way before that.

When **did** it actually begin? When did this acquaintance grow into the friendship, the bond that it became? I think I've heard it compared to a vessel being filled with water a few drops at a time. One drop finally overflows and changes the entire vessel into something of a different, deeper value.

Penny's lovely daughter Becky is a couple of years younger than Melinda, so about four younger than Teresa. We knew each other in Sunday School and church when the girls were young, then when we moved our membership to a church closer to our home, we found that Penny had done that same thing. So we knew each other in two churches and we really lived in close proximity to each other too.

Our youth group was comprised of grades seven through twelve, so the girls had some contact with each other there. I knew Penny to be a decent person by observing her work in the church. She was 100% behind the youth program, enjoyed helping with children's Bible drill, and had a gift with helping out the elderly and other shut-ins (visiting, taking food, etc.). She regularly took a turn in the church nursery too. Our lives bumped into each other's fairly frequently.

I took on the church library sometime within those years and when I needed a helper, Penny volunteered. I began to learn her heart and she was a great listener to **my** heart. She let me be me and I let her be her, yet we had an impact on each other and a charisma with each other that pushed each of us into those "larger selves," I like to think. Sometimes I learned some of the good she did for others that nobody else knew – she wouldn't let me tell because she really thought that God knowing was enough. (Too many others knowing might diminish the ultimate reward of that, she would say.)

To Penny I could voice my praises, my discouragement, my frustration, my longings, my hopes, and sometimes, I'm sorry to say, my hopelessness about one thing or another. She always seemed to know how to listen and she put lots of thought into the words of advice she gave.

Penny loved homemade cookies and I baked a batch to share with her occasionally. One night in the midst of Teresa's journey I remember bringing cookies to Penny and while she ate them I began to talk. I prefaced my conversation with, "I probably shouldn't feel this way, but... Maybe I shouldn't even voice it...."

And Penny looked up at me with a slight concerned frown and in a voice heavy with cookie crumbs, exclaimed, "Hey, it's meeeee!" I didn't need to be reminded after that conversation that I could say anything to her.

While Penny might not be comfortable teaching a class or being in front of a large group, she has extraordinary business and organizational strengths. She doesn't mind approaching people about matters that need tending to. And she has a practical approach to life and a determination to make a difference wherever she can. She CARES. Most importantly I need to say she has a strong reliance on the Lord and a very direct way of talking to Him.

When Teresa and Bradley decided to marry, Penny said, knowing that our medical bills had been high and money was not too plentiful, "I think the ladies of this church would want to give Teresa her reception as a wedding gift." I was flabbergasted and began to vehemently protest this suggestion. Becky and another young woman friend of Teresa's were already buying bridesmaid's dresses. We had already felt so much love and support from all of our friends at Oakwood, it just seemed beyond what I could fathom. Penny begged me to just let her "ask a few people."

What happened after that was an astonishing downpour of God's amazing grace and love on the Edwardses and Taylors. Gallons of punch, cheese balls, meat balls, sandwiches, dip, fruit trays, lace tablecloths, decorations, hours of labor... There was no adequate way we could ever say thank you. I made a little rhyme to send out to folks by way of thanks:

Jesus fed a crowd of folks
With a little boy's lunch
And after they were finished
They knew they'd been loved "a bunch."
Our friends took some of this same love
And fed another crowd,
And afterwards our family felt
So humbled, yet so proud.
How did we deserve to have
Such splendid friends as you,
To help us make Teresa's plans
And hopes and dreams come true?
All we envisioned and even more,
It was the answer to a prayer.
Just know that we don't ever forget
The ways you showed you care!

Penny had the vision for this endeavor and I think there was a blessing for so many in the accomplishment of it.

When Teresa's heart began to fail Penny made sure that she was always there for us – with her physical presence but with a prayer presence too. She and her husband Ronny had built a small garden fish pond in their backyard and they were the ones who encouraged Terry to start on ours. As mentioned earlier in this story, it was such therapy for him and for Teresa near the time of her surgery.

Penny helped me think through insurance matters, how much to press the doctors for various needs, and how to get organized when the transplant neared. She took on the job of "phone list master." She asked for the numbers of those we wanted to notify when we got the call that a donor heart was available. She had work, home, and mobile numbers for a host of people, many of whom she did not yet know. She made sure I had all of the numbers where I could reach her at all hours.

Penny got the pastor for us the night we left for MUSC. She and Ronny came over to our house too. Then she was among those who made the trip to be there with us during that night. Becky had married Bobby by this time and he drove them and our friend Chris Bradley. They stayed on into the day of Teresa's transplant. Ronny is a trucker and he had to make a run to Charleston the next day. After his delivery he parked his big rig somewhere in the city and came over to the hospital. Sometimes I have trouble parking my **car** in the city, so I really marveled at his successful efforts to get there!

When Penny returned to Lexington she checked on our house twice a day. We had Teresa's dog Zack there until he could come to Charleston, Melinda's cocker spaniel Lily and our old poodle Taffy. Our yard was not fenced at that time but Penny has a way with animals and twice a day she let the three of them out and never lost one of them. She checked on the pond, fed the fish, and fed Charlie the cat too. After the first several days of Teresa's recovery had passed, Terry came home to work during the week and returned to Charleston on weekends. Penny brought food every single day for him and left it in our refrigerator. She took the plates from the previous day away. (Terry did wash them up for her each night!) Every single day she did this. Occasionally Becky or Penny's mother, who was a delightful, attractive, God-loving, outspoken, mischievous, fun-loving senior member of our church would come with her. One day Lily, our cocker spaniel, jumped in the open car door right into Mrs. Virginia's lap. (She was waiting there while Penny accomplished her chores with the animals.) She was surprised but not unhappily so. She enjoyed telling about Lily's spontaneity. And Mrs. Virginia had to be proud of Penny's faithfulness in doing good for us and so many others that I know she has helped, never ever "growing weary in well-doing."

In the midst of this Penny still took time to listen to me when I called. When one scary thing after another happened she always knew what to say. She took all of our requests to prayer meeting. One night I told her I didn't even know how to pray. She said, "You go to sleep tonight saying "Lord, I need your help. Lord, I need your help. Lord, I need your help. This will work!" It did. Whatever crisis we had, God solved it once again. The next night I would go to bed saying, "Thank you, Lord. Thank you, Lord. Thank you, Lord. Thank you...."

What a blessing to have a friend who celebrates, grieves, confides, listens, gives, receives, advises, prays, empathizes, sympathizes, understands, and loves unconditionally. It must have been that God, as He was thinking through the creation process, decided, "Let there be friendship. May it be a great shining symbol of the love I have for these my children." And there was created the woman Penny. And the morning and the evening were a good day, a bright day. She is a brilliant representative of those who loved us through.

No sir. I wouldn't take a trillion dollars for my Penny.

Chapter 18 Go Home to Thy Friends

Go home to thy friends, and tell them how great things the Lord hath done for thee." Mark 5:10 (KJV)

Teresa basked in the warmth and light and joy of her recovery. Yes, there were regular trips to Charleston. There were the initial biopsies and she knew that every year on the transplant anniversary there would be a "routine" heart cath. Almost every medical visit required a blood draw to monitor her medicines and her health. Adjustments were made as dictated by lab results and any symptoms she was having. Just as a sample of these adjustments, at one doctor visit my journal entry states: Decrease Vasotec to 5mg. once a day; decrease Cellcept to 1250 twice a day; decrease Prednisone to 10 mg. once a day; discontinue iron; decrease Pepcid to 1 a day; increase Neoral to 4 in AM and 3 in PM; change from Benadryl to Claritin. This was once again a new normal for us. Yes, her immunity was low and we were on constant watch about that. We (particularly **I**) went on alert if there was the slightest fever or rise in blood pressure or heart rate. She was supposed to wear a paper medical mask in those initial months, and she usually did this for doctors' visits or in a big crowd, especially during flu season. Teresa was feeling so much more like a normal person, though, that as soon as she could she shed the mask. And yes, there were dietary and exercise suggestions that were fairly stringent.

Despite these "yeses" which might seem burdensome to a normally healthy person, the biggest YES Teresa saw was the YES to getting on with living this new chance at health and happiness and productivity. She wanted to let everyone know how much this chance meant and she wanted to tell them about what a great gift she had received, how she valued the support she had received. Several examples of how she did this come clearly to mind.

Those last several months before transplant Teresa had shopped from that wheel chair. One day we were wheeling her through the aisles and checkout of the local Piggly Wiggly store. The young woman cashier just couldn't seem to believe that someone so young and seemingly, on the surface, healthy had to be confined to that chair. Her very honest, curious question was, "What happened?" thinking, I feel sure looking back, that there had been some crippling accident. Teresa was not the least bit offended by her question and took the time to answer and to tell her that she might be a candidate for a heart transplant in the near future. The interest and concern in the young woman's face touched Teresa. A few weeks after she got home and we were passing by the grocery store, Teresa stopped me, "Here. The Piggly Wiggly. I want to go in and show our cashier how well I am now." We did, and it meant as much to Teresa as to the young woman who had expressed her concern.

Anna Marie Richardson, a young girl in our church, had taken a liking to and interest in Teresa and it was a mutual affinity. Every time Anna Marie saw Teresa at church she came and gave her a hug. This kindness Teresa never ever forgot. Although years younger than Teresa, Anna Marie was definitely on Teresa's list of friends. Anna Marie reminded me not so long ago of a doll that Teresa gave her and that she still had in her possession so many years later. "A little child shall lead them..." Isaiah 11:6 (NKJV) Never think a child is too young to have an influence for good. And to all supervising, influencing adults, please never let a child think that either!

Bruce Rentz, an adult in our church who had had a kidney transplant, was another who encouraged Teresa and our family when she returned home. Bruce had received his kidney years earlier and had done extremely well. He would go on to keep that kidney way over twenty years, ultimately struggling with even bigger health issues than the transplant and persevering against great odds for a long time. This brave man was in our corner and we enjoyed sharing successes with him.

Because she had been encouraged and restored to health, and wanting to pay that forward, Teresa became interested in encouraging others who might be candidates for heart transplant. Mr. Charles Rollins was from Saluda, South Carolina, and Teresa nudged him along until he was transplanted in February of 2001. She visited him in Charleston before he was transplanted, after his transplant, and they rode in a parade together in Saluda county in 2002 after both of them were living the dream of reclaimed health. Precious little Mrs. Mary Pearce was another dear patient that Teresa was determined to encourage. Just a delightful, joy-filled life-lover, Mary got her heart, as I recall, a little over a year after Teresa was transplanted, which thrilled Teresa. While these three did not often see each other as their lives resumed, Teresa never lost them from her heart and memory and whenever their names came up, we rejoiced in their good fortune along with ours.

One other big project that brought Teresa so much happiness in sharing her experiences was one that her Aunt Betty suggested. Betty was teaching at Gilbert Elementary School and her elementary students took Teresa on to encourage, writing her letters while she was in Charleston and asking her questions. As Teresa began to feel better, even before she permanently returned to Lexington, she wanted to write to Betty's class. Later, when she got home, she would continue her contact with them. I found the letter that she wrote to them from Charleston. It shows a bit of her life perspective, her thoughts on her illness and on her recovery up to that point.

Dear Friends:

Hello! I hope that you are all having a good day. I really enjoyed reading the letters that you wrote me.

Since you all told me a little bit about yourselves, let me tell you a little bit more about me. I am 25 years old and my birthday is August 12, 1975. I live on Calks Ferry Road in Lexington, but I am closer to the town of Gilbert. I have lived in the Columbia/ Lexington area all of my life. I grew up mostly in the Oak Grove section of Lexington. My mother is the librarian at White Knoll Middle School. My dad is a barber and owns a salon in West Columbia, and I have a sister who is 22 years old and lives in Columbia and goes to college. They are all doing well. I have lots of friends from school and church. They have come to see me and have been calling to check on me since I have been in Charleston.

I have been married for about two years and three months. My husband's name is Bradley and he works for his dad at Taylor's Auto Sales in Lexington. Bradley likes to race cars at the race track and he takes karate classes in Gilbert at Shotokan Karate near the railroad tracks. I also have a dog named Zack. He is a Chihuahua and is into everything.

I graduated from Lexington High School in 1993 and from Midlands Technical College in December of 1998 with an Associate's Degree in Office Systems Technology. I did like school, but I didn't like homework. YUCK! My favorite subject had to be computers because that is mostly what I work with in my job. I worked as a legal secretary for the Law Offices of Frederick I. Hall, III in Lexington for about 3 years and for an accountant, John Todd, CPA during tax season last year. I plan to go back to work.

My favorite things to do right now are eating and going shopping, both of which I couldn't do before. I especially like to eat out in the restaurants, but now that I have a new heart I have to eat low fat, low sodium, low cholesterol, and low sugar. That cuts out about all the good stuff, huh? Bradley says that I have made up for lost time in shopping. I think I wore him out at the mall. My favorite sport is football. I don't play a sport because my old heart wouldn't let me, but I enjoy watching football. I hope I get to go to a Carolina football game this year (another thing I couldn't do before) and I hope they win.

When I was 12 years old I was diagnosed with hypertrophic cardiomyopathy. This means that I had a very thick and stiff heart muscle that made it hard for my heart to pump the blood. Yes, I was told that I had a big heart but I don't know exactly how big. When I was first told that I had this heart disease not much changed except that I had to quit P.E. and other physical activity. I was dancing at the time and had to quit that too. I did notice that I couldn't do as much as the other kids my age. I would get short of breath if I did too much. Other than that I didn't have many symptoms at first, so when I was told of the heart disease it really didn't affect me emotionally because I could still do most of the same things I was doing before. The people who knew that I had a weak heart didn't treat me any differently. They just knew that I may not be able to walk as far as they could and would have to take a rest along the way. As time progressed, my symptoms got worse.

The doctors at the National Institutes of Health in Maryland said that I was in the last stages of the heart disease about 3 years ago. They said that my heart had a chance of going into ventricular fibrillation, which is a dangerous heart rhythm. My doctor here suggested that I get a defibrillator implanted in my chest that would shock my heart out of this dangerous rhythm since the chance was there and this would take care of that problem. So I got the defibrillator and it did shock my heart a couple of times and yes it hurt and scared me. I would say that for the past 2-3 years I have felt pretty bad. I got to where I couldn't eat or sleep. I lost a lot of weight. I was scared that the defibrillator would shock me again. I would get very dizzy if I had to walk anywhere and was in a wheelchair most of the time. I had a chronic cough and my muscles and joints ached a lot of the time. And, I was gaining a lot of fluid in my legs and stomach. I had to move to my mom's house this past April so that she could take care of me while my husband worked. This is when my doctor decided that I did need a heart transplant.

When I found out that I needed a heart transplant I had mixed feelings. I was scared first of all but knew it was what I needed to do. My mom said, "You will feel so much better. You have forgotten what it feels like to be well." I was told many success stories about other people who had received heart transplants. Everyone was so positive that it made me think more positive too.

I got my new heart at the Medical University of South Carolina in Charleston on July 24. I had to wait a while on the doctors because they had to go get my new heart. They were travelling to get it in a storm and things kept getting delayed. The wait wasn't too bad though because I had about 20 family members and friends there to support me. I had the surgery on Monday and they say I began to wake up on Tuesday. I don't remember anything that happened until Saturday. And, Conner, I think I was on a little more than laughing gas. I was told that I said some pretty crazy things.

That Saturday, that first day that I remember, I was still in the intensive care unit. I was still kind of out of it. I was in intensive care for seven days in all and then moved to a regular room for another seven days. While I was in the hospital I wasn't really scared because I knew that if something happened to my new heart that they could take care of it.

I do have to take a lot of medication. I take some medicine that shuts down my immune system and keeps my body from rejecting my heart because it doesn't recognize it as part of me. This is the same as you catching a cold and your body fighting it off. My body could recognize this new heart as something bad and try to fight it off or reject it. Because my immune system is shut down, I also have some medicine that keeps me from catching a virus such as chicken pox. I also take vitamins because some of my medicine takes things out of my body that I need such as iron, potassium, and magnesium. And then I take medicine to soothe my stomach because some of my medicine can irritate it. I am taking a lot of medication right now, but will eventually be able to come off of some of it.

Since I have gotten my new heart I feel so much better. I have been shopping at the mall, the market, Steinmart, Marshalls, and Barnes and Noble. I spend my days going to physical therapy for an hour, looking at the heart healthy cookbooks, going shopping, and exercising. Before my new heart I could only walk for 2 minutes on the treadmill and now I walk for 30 minutes twice a day. That is a little more than 2 miles. I am also exercising on a stepper for about 5 minutes but have to go longer before I can graduate from physical therapy. I go to the hospital once every two weeks to meet with the doctors so they can see how I am doing. When they say I am well enough and when I complete my physical therapy, I can go home. I will finish physical therapy in about 3 weeks and hope that they will let me go then. It just depends on the doctors and how I am doing at that time.

It was nice to hear from all of you. Please keep remembering me in your prayers. The Lord has gotten me this far and isn't going to let anything bad happen to me now. And, yes, I am feeling great and am happy to have a new heart and new life.

Your friend with a new heart,
Teresa Taylor

So that letter was the beginning of a friendship with Aunt Betty's class that was to continue to be an encouragement as she came home to "tell her friends what great things the Lord had done for her!" She didn't miss an opportunity to let others know what a gift she had received, especially in those early years of her renewed health.

Chapter 19 More of Year One

Teresa went all out for the Christmas season in 2000. She went to productions of "A Christmas Carol," "The Singing Christmas Tree" (in which her local cardiologist was a part of the choir), "The Grinch Who Stole Christmas," and "This Man Called Jesus." She spoke to her Aunt Betty's class, in person this time, and co-hosted the school news program at the school that day. She had fifteen people at her house/yard for a hot dog roast one night. She had her house ablaze with inside and outside Christmas lights. This was such a contrast to the somber air of the prior year's season.

As Teresa's heart biopsies became more infrequent, the transplant team suggested that she be seen in Charleston by Dr. Van Bakel every six months and by Dr. Beard locally every six months. By staggering these appointments, someone would be checking on things every three months. She did have a six months appointment at MUSC in January that involved a biopsy, stress test, echocardiogram, bone density test, and chest x-ray. Her liver enzymes were up slightly and they discontinued her Zocor and planned to recheck for those numbers in four weeks. Except for that and for changing the dosages of a couple of other medicines, the visit was uneventful, which was good.

They had not been able to take Teresa's defibrillator out during the transplant surgery. While they had cut the leads and she had a head full of knowing that it could not shock her, she was still eager to "get that thing out of there." They agreed to this of course and on March 2, 2001 we went to MUSC to have that done. Before the procedure Teresa wanted to visit some of those who had helped her along the way and she visited Paris, a nurse in Intensive Care, Paula, the dietician, and Sue Ellen, the financial counselor. She loved it when they all told her how well she seemed to be doing. It always bolstered her courage for the next event.

She was an add-on for the surgical procedure, and we understood there would be a wait. It was a couple of hours after we arrived before they were able to take her back, then after work-up it was another couple of hours before they took her to surgery. Bradley and I were getting worried about 3:30 and I inquired at the desk. They told me that Dr. Crumbley was still operating but that if we had not heard by 4:00 they would call into the operating room. I still ask God to forgive me for never getting used to "the wait" throughout those years after her initial diagnosis, the sense of dread and trying to prepare myself for bad news. Sometimes my own broken heart felt that it would give out and I would try to remember that God does not give us a spirit of fear. This was not just during surgical procedures but almost any time a doctor came into the room with us. I am ashamed now, but here is the truth of it: I was terrified of more bad news even as I rejoiced in the miraculous restoration of her health.

Teresa did make it through the removal of that defibrillator just fine, despite the nervousness she felt ahead of it. She told us her heart had been skipping or pounding or "something" all week, particularly at night, and I feel sure it was anxiety about the surgery. They gave the defibrillator to her after they removed it. She had said she wanted to throw it off the Folly Beach pier, but of course she did not do that.

Sitting in the waiting room that day was humbling. Almost always at MUSC, or at any hospital in fact, you can find others who are struggling with terrible medical issues. On this day we were with a family whose loved one/patient was having a 15-hour surgery related to cancer. Another family with a handicapped daughter were waiting through her 22nd surgery. Then in the holding room for the OR, there was a lady in the next bed with two aneurysms who was headed for serious emergency surgery. The army of healers was busy and the Great Physician was surely busy sending them directions on March 2, 2001.

We had spent the night in Charleston and the next day Teresa wanted to go and see Charles Rollins, our friend from Saluda who had just gotten his transplant a couple of weeks earlier and was still recovering in Charleston. She said, "He may say, 'Why did you encourage me to do this? They have ruined me!"

We asked her if she had felt that way. She said, "At first I did. I thought, 'What have they done to me? I'm swollen. I have the shakes. I can't even hold my body up.'" She wanted Charles to know that if he did feel like that, it would pass. We found Charles with his wife carefully watching over him. I remember taking their picture and marveling once again at the miracle of their two lives.

Teresa had a puncture in one lung during a biopsy that spring but there was no lasting damage, just again a fear that there would be. They had cautioned her, "If shortness of breath develops, go to the local emergency room and say the word "'pneumothorax.'" She still had some elevated liver enzymes that they watched carefully and there was some concern about some enlarged lymph nodes (adenopathy) near her pancreas. All in all, though, things were progressing toward the heart cath that was scheduled during the summer to see how everything was at year one.

We continued to meet patients who were at various stages of transplantation. At the MUSC fundraiser in April, we met a lady with three children who began having heart attacks after her third baby. She was transplanted when her baby was nine months old. Another lady with two daughters ages fourteen and seventeen had been transplanted in March of 1999. She had had some rejection early on and was still taking some fairly high doses of one of the immunosuppressants. Then there was a 54-year-old who had gotten a heart and kidney in 1999 and a lady who had had her heart thirteen years – the first woman transplanted at MUSC. Everyone was so positive and I smile when I look at the pictures we took that day.

They did a CT scan during that summer of 2001 to check on that adenopathy. It came back okay for that and they figured it had probably been due to the heart failure Teresa had experienced prior to transplant. BUT they also saw some scarring near the lung/breast area and wanted to keep check on that. There would always be things to pop up like this, we came to know, but Teresa just learned to live her life around these events, always, always clinging to the good times, the normal times, the chance to do the things she loved.

The heart cath that summer showed that the heart was functioning perfectly, the valves were clear and the pressures were good. We threw a one-year anniversary party in the fellowship hall of our church and so many of our friends and supporters were there to share it with us.

PART THREE

Chapter 20 The Glory Years

They had told Teresa that the four things that could cause problems for transplant patients sooner or later were heart failure, coronary artery disease, infections, and cancer. She was told about what kinds of things to look out for. She did not worry as much as I did. She had some burping and reflux problems and cramping stomachaches from time to time during 2002. They adjusted her acid reflux medicine. They put her back on Asacol for the ulcerative colitis. The heart cath in 2002 showed fairly normal pressures and normal vessels.

Since her liver enzymes were still slightly up they wanted to biopsy her liver to be sure it was okay for her to take the statin drugs which helped regulate cholesterol, so they did that in early 2003 the same day that they did the heart biopsy. (She was still having these done in January of 2003.) I remember Dr. Van Bakel being pleased when she told him during that visit that she was going to the gym and doing about 45 minutes of cardio and 45 minutes of weights.

I also wrote in my journal that in August of 2003 she was taking about 15 medicines and/or supplements, either prescription or over-the-counter. It was about 30 or so pills a day. Since the liver biopsy had come back okay they felt it was safe to put her back on the statin drug Lipitor, as her LDL had begun to creep up a bit. This was the drug they had stopped when her liver enzyme reading was higher than they liked it. It was also during 2003 that Teresa began to have panic attacks and Xanax was prescribed for that. She had always been the calmest of children and even as a teenager never seemed to be flustered or bothered by much, so none of us could understand when she developed this. I came to realize that no one is immune to this condition. She would feel like she could not breathe, her heart would pound, her chest would feel heavy, and sometimes the feeling of pressure would run up her shoulders, neck, and jaw. There was no question she needed help with it, as she felt when she was in the midst of these attacks that she was having a heart attack.

Even with all of the doctoring and drugs, Teresa continued to marvel at her life. She had gotten a beautiful letter from her donor's family in July of 2003. Teresa wanted to convey to them her thanks and the words that she wrote to them will always be a treasure to me, as they describe so well her perceptions of her renewed life. I have removed the donor's name and those of her children from this letter, but they stay inside my heart always, very near to where I keep my own strong, sweet girl.

August 17, 2003
Dear Donor Family,

What a blessing I received on July 6, 2003, the day that I received your letter in my mailbox. Over the past three years I have often thought of you and (donor's name), and what she must have been like. It is so sad for me to think of the loss of such a young person, a daughter, a mother in your lives. You still have my deepest sympathy for I know that her loss will never be easy for you.

What an extraordinarily generous, loving, and strong family you must be to have given the heart of your loved one that you lost to save the life of a complete stranger. (Donor's children), I understand that it was your decision to donate your mother's organs. What a difficult decision for you to make and what a dramatic difference it has made in my life. You will never know how grateful I am to you for the life that God has given to me through you.

Thank you so much for the letter that you sent me. I am so glad to get to know about (Donor's name's) life and to get the picture of your family. I didn't know anything about my donor or their family until you sent the letter. It was truly a joy! What a beautiful lady she was inside and out. (Donor's sons) are such handsome young men and (Donor's daughter) such a pretty young lady. I know you all loved and adored her and she loved you all too. I can tell by the way you wrote of her in your letter.

My mother wrote to you soon after my transplant 3 years ago. She told you how sick I was and how close to death I was becoming. I had just turned 25 then and was still recovering from my surgery. I now have just turned 28 (August 12), had my three-year heart cath and biopsy and am feeling better than I had ever dreamed I would.

*I live a pretty regular lifestyle. I have been married to my high school sweetheart, best friend, and most wonderful husband for five years now. I have a Chihuahua named Zack who is spoiled rotten - he gets too many "tweats" as we call them - and he knows what that word means. He's a little overweight and you can probably imagine why. I work forty hours a week at an attorney's office in the Real Estate Closing Department. (We've been really busy lately with the low interest rates.) And when I get off work at 5:30, I go to the GYM and do lots of exercising! Bradley, my husband, and I go to the same gym. Bradley is into bodybuilding and I do cardio and some weight training. Then we go home and cook supper, watch TV, and go to bed....then, get up and do it all over again the next day. The weekends are more laid back. We really enjoy spending time together and going on small trips occasionally. We go to church on Sundays where I have been a member since middle school. The people there are like my family and have really stuck by me. I hope to get involved in helping with the AWANA program this year. I think that will really be a blessing....and last but not least, I have the BEST Mama, Daddy and younger sister that anyone could wish for. I love them so much and treasure every opportunity I get to spend with them. I just live a normal everyday routine that many people take for granted and that I thank GOD for everyday that I am able to live. I feel so good. I LOVE life!! I LOVE **my** life!!*

Once again, you will never know the enormous difference that you have made in my life. I know that God has a plan for everyone and that not a one of us is promised tomorrow. I am living my new life and enjoying it. I am taking good care of your loved one's heart and it is taking good care of me. I pray for your family often and know that God will bless you indeed!! Thank you for the gift of life that you have given to me!!

Love to you all,
Teresa

I cannot describe any plainer than Teresa's own words what it meant for her to be in the world and in her life as she was during these "glory years." This little poem did occur to me as I reflected on Isaiah

40:31 and saw her awakening to all of the possibilities that were now available to her.

"...they that wait upon the Lord shall renew their strength; they shall mount up with wings as eagles; they shall run and not be weary; and they shall walk, and not faint." Isaiah 40: 31 (KJV)

Can it be these are the wings
Of which the prophet sings?
These wings...
so long denied the skies
of my small world.

And are these legs to run
A race just now begun
on this
vast space of track...
now mine to own?

What an analogy to life, the race. Endurance, timing, the track, the racers, and the finish line! And different kinds of races in different terrains, in various seasons, of varying lengths. Indeed, I will run and not be weary; I will walk, and not faint. Teresa's mantra.

Chapter 21 Dreams of Motherhood

Teresa had accomplished two of her life goals – marrying Bradley and finishing her degree at Midlands Technical College – before her transplant. Staying alive and staying as well as possible became her goals throughout the transplant process. Then her goal immediately after, and for those first couple of years after, was to attain that manageable "normal for her" routine which would hopefully sustain and enrich her life for many years to come. When she felt she had reached that place she pushed for what was to become, next to joining her life with Bradley's, the one thing she had always yearned for more than anything else in the world. She wanted a child to complete her family, "a baby in my arms, Mama, a baby in my arms." In late 2003 and early 2004, as she was doing all of the things described in her letter to her donor's family, she gave herself to pursuing this dream.

Teresa was not sure how God was going to deliver this baby, whether biologically or through adoption, but she began to ask Him. We may not have always recognized it, but He answered clearly through those he put in her life at this time. She began by going to MUSC to talk to them about the possibility of giving birth. We had read about transplant patients who had delivered babies, but heart recipients not as often as kidney or even liver recipients. After going over all of her medical history and her present, mostly good health status, her doctors said to her, "If you want to do this, we will do everything we know to help you, but we don't recommend it." There were risks to both mother and child, particularly from the immunosuppressive drugs and also the increased chance of hypertension, infection, etc.

Teresa seemed to know and accept at once then that her child would not be born biologically but would be delivered from deep inside the heart of God into **her** heart, her arms, and her family. This is in fact what happened and He used Teresa's beloved pastor from the days of her adolescence at Oakwood to accomplish this. Steve and Lynn Eargle had loved Teresa for a number of years by this time. They had moved to an Anderson church from Lexington and as they were ministering there God called them to direct their own adoption agency. They were working with international adoptions and had in fact helped Bradley's uncle and aunt adopt three children into their family. They had increased their own family through multiple adoptions and had great big loving, compassionate, energetic hearts that beat for kids. When Lynn and Steve learned that Teresa longed for a child, they stepped up and wanted to help her with a domestic adoption and explained the process to her and Bradley.

Their first task was to compile a portfolio of their lives which was to include facts about the history of their relationship, their occupations, their interests, their dreams, their passions, their religious preference, their means, their belief and statement on why they wanted a child and what they wanted **for** that child. Prospective adoptive parents' portfolios would be presented to prospective biological moms and those that matched her desires would be selected for further investigation. Teresa threw herself into this with her whole heart, this realistic portrayal of their family contained between the covers of a lovingly prepared scrapbook. She was determined that there would be no doubt to anyone that their child would be coming to two very real people who had loved each other a long time, certainly not without adversity, but longing to impart to a child a sense of family, faith, unconditional love, devotion, loyalty, and just the fun and joy of being together in this unbroken circle. When she was satisfied that this had been accomplished in her effort, she gave her portfolio over to Steve and Lynn and waited. She was not sure how long the wait would be but she knew it would be worth it.

I don't remember the date of that late winter or early spring day, but I never forget the moment that Teresa called me to say, "Someone has picked us." I was standing in the office of my school library when the phone rang. There was a calm (calm always being a part of her demeanor, it seemed), yet contained excitement in her voice, an awe, a wonderment, a praise. There was expectation there, with an attempt at tempering that expectation with the realization that it might not work, that things happen in the process sometimes. But her delight in the accomplishment of this first step, this first hurdle to meet the baby God was going to give her was a joy to everyone who knew and loved Teresa and Bradley. The excitement never lessened from the moment of that phone call onward.

The next steps involved meeting with Lynn and Steve and the birth mother and some of her family support, determining if this would be a match for all involved, making arrangements for obstetric care, for the mother's other needs during the pregnancy, etc. There were a few bumps, some rough patches along this path, but what I remember overall is a euphoric journey toward a new little person's birth. Teresa and Bradley were involved every step of the way and often included us grandparents in this as well. We laughed and joked and sometimes cried with this other family as we searched their hearts, learned their desires, felt their yearnings, observed their weaknesses and admired their strengths. We wanted to put our best foot forward as we knew they were summing up the possibilities for this new life that was coming into the world, but we also wanted them to know that we were real, genuine, and ready to provide as real and genuine a life as possible for this chosen child. October 2004 was to be a magical month.

The months leading up to October were full of trips to the upcountry, corresponding with Lynn and Steve and the mom, shopping with her and going to some of her doctor's appointments with her. The other big joyful task for Teresa and Bradley was outfitting the room that would be the nursery. They had decided that if a girl, the baby would be named for Bradley's grandmother and great-grandmother. If a boy, they would name him for Teresa's grandfathers. When we found out he was a boy, we knew him as Preston Henry Taylor, to be called Preston. In our hearts rang the psalmist's words, "My cup runneth over." Psalm 23: 5b (KJV)

Chapter 22 Scared

We had a scare in the summer of 2004. While we never got used to Teresa's heart caths or found them routine, we did mostly know what to expect by this time. She was scheduled for the yearly cath on July 27, 2004. We got there at 9:00 but she did not actually go into the procedure until 11:15. We knew about the preliminaries involving blood work, vital signs, setting of the IV line, consent forms, etc. and sometimes there were emergencies or other holdups for a cath lab. There was a very nice young doctor, a resident I believe, who consented Teresa that day. He seemed quite fatigued though. MUSC is a teaching hospital and often the residents assisted with procedures, and if far enough along in their training, could perform procedures with an attending physician's supervision. They told us it would be about one to one and a half hours.

Usually, after a procedure was over, the doctor who performed it would step out into the waiting area, let us know initial findings and tell us that when she got back to recovery we could see her. We were becoming uneasy about 1:00 when a volunteer came out to say that the doctor wanted to see us in the consultation room. I remember sitting down in that little room and thinking, "This is not usual." I began searching my heart and the scriptures there and then from my mouth I heard, "I will lift up mine eyes unto the hills, from whence cometh my help. My help cometh from the Lord, which made heaven and earth." Psalm 121:1-2 (KJV) I could feel my own heart rate and breathing speed up. The doctor arrived after a short wait and commented that the look on our faces told him we didn't know that they routinely called families to the consult room. We certainly didn't know, as we had never been called into one before like this! He then reported on what had occurred, which was not at all routine.

During the cath they saw a small clot begin to form in a branch of a small blood vessel. They thought the clot had formed on the end of the catheter during the procedure. They probed it through and it dissipated, but Dr. Van Bakel wanted to watch her overnight. She was given heparin in a drip to prevent further clots from forming. They would do another enzyme check to be sure there had not been an "assault" on the heart. When Dr. Van Bakel came by a bit later, his theory was that the clot was probably dye-related, that the dye **had** clumped on the end of the catheter. He did not think she was forming clots on a regular basis. He did want to do enzyme level checks to see if there was any residual damage. They drew blood at 11:30 and 1:00 to begin checking those enzymes that are indicators.

On the morning of July 28 a doctor we had not seen before came by to say that yes, the enzymes showed that there had been a slight injury to the heart, or a "mild heart attack." The good news was that it would probably not affect heart function and would probably not show up on a stress test. Dr. Van Bakel described it as the corner of a big steak being overdone or charred a bit. He told her too that her heart function overall should continue to be effective and that she did not need to let it affect her psychologically and keep her from doing and planning as she usually did. She could return to work and exercise in a week. He did want to keep her another day.

When they told us the risks before each heart cath, they always included "a small percentage risk of stroke, heart attack, bleeding...." Before later caths, when they recited those lines, Teresa would tell them, "I already contributed to fulfilling the risk factor on that one, so I don't want or expect another round of it!" Funny, but not.

Teresa did get back into her life. While she did not forget the experience, ever, she did not let it keep her from moving forward to some of the best years of her life.

Chapter 23 More than Glory Years

Teresa's story could never be complete without attempting to describe the boy that she and Bradley brought into their family. I feel that this chapter of her memoir will be inadequate, underdone, lacking, because there are no words that I have read or heard that can completely describe the joy that Preston's birth brought to her and Bradley and to ALL of their family on both sides. Anyone reading who loves a child will, I hope, feel our happiness in your heart close to where you keep **your** own dear ones.

October 26, 2004 was a carefully planned day. Preston would arrive by Caesarean section. Steve and Lynn, some of the birth family, and Teresa and Bradley's families were there. We spoke with the birth mom beforehand and then immediately after the surgery we were able to be in the hospital room when they came back there. Preston was small but absolutely healthy. He had a red birthmark on one of his arms, the kind that fades with age, and it was perfectly shaped like a heart. When I looked into his beautiful little face the first words I knew to say were, "You are beyond poetry and past symphonies." I know every grandparent thinks that God has had His finest creative moment in designing his/her grandchild. Terry and I and Drayton and Nella were surely in that category. We pampered and soothed his birth mother, rejoiced with his adoptive mother and daddy, and in our hearts felt fireworks of gratitude, love, and yes, we felt the big responsibility that lay ahead.

Preston went home with Teresa and Bradley the next day. I remember being in Belk the night before shopping for preemie clothes. He did not wear these for long, but the things Teresa had brought were too big she thought, so we went on the search for something to fit him. Just as I felt when our daughters had been born to Terry and me, Preston Henry Taylor was a doll in **her** arms and a praise in **her** heart. The next night when we came to Lexington with him, Teresa and Bradley's cousins and friends had prepared the way. Jody and Teresa Miller had placed Welcome Words on the big sign outside the Big J Ranch store that they owned nearby. Teresa's coworkers were at her house with their welcoming arms and hugs and oohs and aahs. They laid Preston down to sleep in the little boy's room so lovingly readied for him, with treasures made possible again by the generous showers and gifts of friends and family.

Some of you may be asking these questions: Why did Teresa want to bring a child into her life when her health was not guaranteed? Was that selfish? Wasn't she afraid that she might not live to see her child grow up? Teresa had such an optimistic outlook about things in those days, basically all of her days. She had said early on after her transplant, "I am going to do everything they say because I want to be one of the longest-living heart transplants they have ever had." She meant to be here, to raise this child to adulthood. While she knew she had been through a grueling battle to get to her new life, she felt she would get a second transplant if her first one were to begin to fail. She would do it all over again if necessary to stay in the race and to love and launch her own son or daughter into his or her own independence.

There was a waiting period before Preston's adoption became final. That day at the courthouse and afterward at lunch with Steve and Lynn and our family was another celebration of all that was right in the world. This little boy who had captured Teresa's heart and even physically looked like her with his blue blue eyes and fair complexion could not have been more hers and Bradley's by the time his name officially became Preston Henry Taylor.

Teresa was determined to bring the wonnnnnderful to her boy's life as she had described her own childhood to that psychiatrist in her pre-transplant evaluation. She wanted to take him everywhere, and did, beginning when he was only a few days old. She wanted to share him with everyone and it thrilled her when they noticed and loved him. He made a stop at the Fall Festival at our church, visited my childhood friend Sylvia, and was held by countless arms that reached for him in his own home and elsewhere in those early weeks and months. I called him "The Little Prince," not because we thought we were royalty, but because we intended to treasure him as though he were with whatever means we had to do that. While we might have been limited in worldly resources, there was no shortage of love or dotage from those in charge of him. I hope he will always be able to feel how his mother - and all of his family - cherished him, as every child should.

Chapter 24 The WONNNDERFUL of Childhood (Revisited)

Preston never knew the great-grandfathers for whom he was named, but their legacy comes to him through the family that he did get to know. Grandma Tulie Power had Alzheimer's by the time he arrived, but she loved all children and would have adored him. Grandma Clara Edwards did get to love him and we have pictures of their smiling, shining faces together. Aunt Fay and Aunt Lindy covered him with hugs and love. The steadfast Power and Edwards and Taylor uncles, aunts, and cousins who had lovingly pulled us along the way remained stalwartly within our family circle. John Power, J.K. Edwards, and Ann Edwards Heywood would begin to fill their homes, yards and hearts – and ours - with their children and family gatherings became shining, memorable occasions for us all.

Bradley's parents welcomed, in Preston, their first grandchild too. Bradley's paternal grandparents had both passed by the time Preston got here, but GeePa and GeeMa Miller were here. They joined in for Christmas gatherings, family picnics, and fishing excursions. Bradley remembers his grandmother Taylor so lovingly and his great-grandmother "Maw" Miller as a lively, unique little lady who taught children, played piano, and drove to church probably a while after she shouldn't have, but therein, again, lie the family stories, all wound around a small boy who had found his place.

Besides a strong family base, Teresa wanted Preston to have friends and to be a friend and she loved every friend he made through the years. She wanted him to have adventures, to experience the wonder of every holiday as she did, but to find memorable in the ordinary as well. She wanted him to have faith and compassion, to be loving, responsible and respectful. As I began exploring the Preston years I felt drawn to the many thousands of pictures Teresa took throughout her time with him. She shared so many with me and I have tried to keep them all. When I was growing up, my own mother used to say something like, "If this house ever catches fire, after the actual people in it, save the pictures next!" I suppose in this modern age, we will be grabbing our USB drives or counting on "the cloud" for these priceless treasures.

I have seen pictures and videos that take my breath away and back in the day there was no touch-up or editing – what you saw was just the way it was. Teresa did learn the editing software when she got further into her photography hobby, but most of the ones I have are untouched and actually hers are too, but she was able to put together some fantastic video of some of their family trips, a modern miracle of technology. As I started with the pictures of 2004 and moved forward, what I found was that great adventure that childhood should be for any kid, reflected in the little boy dressed as a pumpkin, pirate, clown, Super Mario and various other wonders on Halloween, a shepherd in the Christmas pageant at the Miller family's church, Boiling Springs Methodist, bows and Santa hats and elf costumes on him at family Christmas gatherings, rabbit ears and Easter egg hunts, riding a toy donkey in the church Easter program, a smiling round face smeared with cake frosting on birthdays. He appeared in snapshots at the State Fair, Edventure, Boo at the Zoo, the train museum, Monkey Joe's (where Aunt Fay particularly liked to take him), Broadway at the Beach, fishing at Granddaddy and Nana Taylor's pier at Lake Murray, on the soccer field, at school. There is one of him shucking corn with me in our backyard, naked as he could be at about age two.

Once Teresa called me to alert me that they were sending a picture of him in a toy that they had put together wrong – not to worry despite the look on his face. It was some kind of jumper or rolling thing and instead of being on top and in control he was down inside looking up, not afraid exactly but puzzled maybe about these two laughing adults who had constructed something that had looked like fun on the front of the box but was not producing. He stomped in mud puddles, blew bubbles, took a bath in all kinds of tubs and containers (including the kitchen sink and the hospital dishpan), and tried to walk in Pop's shoes or boots in at least three different snapshots. He played with the pots and pans, climbed onto the door of the dishwasher, played in (and I'm almost sure ate and drank from) the dog's food and water bowls, loved all things that bounced, flew, popped, rolled, slid, swung, fell down, gathered speed, or moved in any direction. He drew, colored, finger-painted, created, and constructed.

In late 2005 Bradley and Teresa made a move into our neighborhood, just across the street from us. How we loved that! Sometimes I ponder and wonder if I helped Teresa enough during the years they lived there. I knew that I was and probably would always be the "mother hen" about her health. What I did not want to do was interfere with the life they had made as a family. I was working fulltime and she was too. Certainly we offered help and we were quite involved in Preston's activities. We loved having him with us. Bradley renovated that house and they made it a lovely place for a small family, not just painting, but opening up walls, installing crown molding, replacing light fixtures, making some plumbing changes and a host of other improvements that caused us to marvel. Preston's room next to theirs was a wonderland and I think they were happy there for those several years. They had rented out their home in the country, knowing, I think, that they might sometime want to return there.

We wanted our backyard to be an inviting place for Preston, so we tried to remember all of the tricks from Teresa and Melinda's childhood: the sandbox, swing set with slide, little swimming pool (and eventually a bigger one), patio picnic table, and room to run around, kick, bounce, hit, swat, and do other things to balls of all sizes. What he loved most as a little child was to run around our big azalea bushes with us chasing. I remember once when he was just about five years old, I said, "Preston, I am getting too old to chase you around these bushes."

He stopped briefly and thoughtfully before replying, "Granna, can you just chase me until your next birthday?" I am thankful that I could still chase him for a long time after that day (albeit slower and inside sometimes!) when we played the silly games that eventually disappeared, except for our memories, into his adolescence.

In one of Teresa's pictures with Preston they are finger-painting together on our back patio. He loved the sloppiness and color and the creative, inventive process, whether with paint, blocks, clay, rocks, sand, or almost any medium. One of his most photographed and cherished creations was an accident most would say, but it held great meaning for us as a family. The little red heart birthmark Preston had as a baby was disappearing as he grew but we did not forget that he came here with that. Teresa also had a tiny heart-shaped spot on her back that was like a freckle in color but shaped precisely like a valentine heart too. On one afternoon, again on the back patio, Preston had decided to play with some tiny gravel rocks and dirt and sand that he scooped up and dumped out. He swirled and smoothed and played in all of that and when he got tired of it he walked away. When we began reminding him to clean up and we looked there at what was left, it was the image of a valentine heart, not precisely defined, yet distinctly identifiable as that. We took pictures immediately and later added the words of I Corinthians 13 to it. It still reminds me that God's love for us and His PLAN for each of us is no accident.

I remember one day when Preston was still small that he and Teresa went down to the back of our yard and in that damp shady corner they dug up some earthworms. The worms on this particular day were not for fishing, just observing, just as he caught bugs and kept them ever so briefly in his little insect cage we had gotten him. He loved digging the worms and the bugs and he loved fishing at the lake but he could not bear for any living creature to die. Any fish he caught in those early years had to be thrown right back while it still had a chance. He cried at any animal that had succumbed to an accident in the highway and when Teresa was driving him somewhere and she saw that, she had to try to distract his attention elsewhere. He loved animals and still does. While he did not get along too famously with Zack-boy the Chihuahua, he did endear himself to the cats that Teresa adopted into the family, Chloe particularly.

Preston's love affair with water began early in his life too. Teresa and Melinda had taken swimming lessons as children and Bradley and his brothers had too. They wanted Preston to feel at home in the water and he seemed to naturally take to it. From bathtub to toddler pool to swimming pool, then to lake and beach he progressed. He got some swimming lessons, and what he did not learn from those, he seemed to get from his own innate fishhood. Aunt Fay taught him to tread water by standing beside the pool and telling him how to do it. Our little above-ground pool thrilled him and he loved it most when someone was in there with him. Pop most often was the lucky one. Since Teresa and Bradley's favorite vacation spot was the beach, he learned to love it there too, both the water and the other activities connected to those trips and being with them there.

It became a tradition for Terry (Pop) and me (Granna) to keep Preston on Sunday nights. How we looked forward to that! We took him to the many parks in Lexington and Columbia, played with him in our backyard, in the little swimming pool, watched him ride whatever wheeled vehicle he was into at any given time, roasted hot dogs and marshmallows, played with play dough, cars, blocks, balls, balloons... I recall clearly an incident that became a life lesson for Pop and me, a reminder of the simple faith of children. We had Preston one summer night when he was little more than a toddler when a thunderstorm came up. The lights began to flicker and I tried to prepare him, catching water, gathering candles, the battery-powered lantern, and other gear. He followed our every step, asking questions about why the lights would go out. We began to hope that maybe our house would be skipped, but sure enough, a loud boom and total darkness. He really had questions then, not liking the situation a bit. I told him I was calling the power company and reporting the power outage and they would get to our area when they could to fix it. We were still scurrying around and his little voice spoke to us in the near-darkness of our candle-lit room, "Has anybody thought to pray?"

I was stunned into silence for a moment before replying, "Well, Preston, that is EXACTLY what we should do. We are going to pray right now." I began to talk to God, "Dear God, please help us in this storm. It's a little scary. Please guide the repairmen to get here as soon as they can."

This was where Preston broke right into the prayer, "And God, they might not get here soon enough. Can YOU just please fix it?" You know, God is ultimately and always our Fixer, even when He does not work on our timetable. That was a powerful lesson from a little boy's heart that night. Never to forget...

Preston enjoyed 'most everything he did when someone else was in the fun with him. He is still that way. He perpetually wants to "just have a friend over." He was a comforter, even in preschool. When someone would get hurt he would give a hug and speak comforting words. Just as Teresa was sensitive to the feelings of others, Preston learned to be too, reading the emotions in others in a way beyond his years. Anytime we told him we were going to take his picture with a friend in those early years, he would fling an arm around the neck of whoever it was beside him. He was good with younger children too as he grew older. Our friendly neighbors Leah and Dan had a smart and lively little daughter Tobin and he and she would play when she came over. He loved spend-the-nights with his pals and when Teresa was able, she encouraged that at their house and then at the homes of others when he was invited. He is still becoming the social creature she envisioned in him. He continues to see his cousins when they gather; he enjoys soccer and the camaraderie with teammates; and he is in close communication with many of his classmates from school. As technology has galloped along, when he is not physically present with a friend he is often connected by phone or computer. His mama would be happy with the friendship involved in all of that.

He loved for Aunt Fay to come and visit. Fay had married Uncle Chalmers in 2006 and occasionally Uncle Chalmers would ride over with Aunt Fay. Uncle Chalmers often had a $5 bill for Preston to put in his wallet. Sometimes Fay would pick him up from preschool or school and take him to the park or to Monkey Joe's, the inflatables gym. Sometimes she would just take him to his house to play. She always brought homemade treats to eat. He never wanted her to leave. Once, when he was still a tiny boy and she was there and beginning to start the good-bye talk, he went around his house and found a collection of things that he thought would block the back door and keep her inside his house. He stacked up in the doorway the mop bucket, broom, mops, and anything of any size that he could carry in hopes of stopping her departure. Anytime his heart broke hers did too. It was that way with all of us. He adored his Aunt Lindy along with Aunt Fay and we only had to mention Melinda's name and he counted himself into every plan that involved her.

Teresa was big on manners and respect. She was constant in her repetition of "Please," "Thank you," "Excuse me," "Yes, Ma'am" and "Yes, Sir." She wanted him to do all the things for himself that he could at every stage of his life. She was after him being responsible and making good choices and taking advantage of the educational opportunities provided in preschool and then in elementary school. She paid attention to the details of every school year, making calendars, purchasing the things he needed, getting his clothes ready, and giving him "pep talks." She made regular pediatrician's appointments, kept up with when lunch money was due, when the yearbooks were arriving, where the field trips would be, what the school tee-shirt choices were, when parents could visit school for various parties and events and what was needed from parents. She enrolled him in Vacation Bible School in the summers and looked for other programs of interest. This attention to detail encompassed his sports teams and schedules too. She always wanted to be a part of every activity that mattered to him.

So progressed Teresa, Bradley, and Preston's life with each other and with their extended families. Was it carefree every minute? No. Is anyone's life? But what she experienced in those happy, healthy, hectic years with her young family can only be described, and would, I believe, be described by her as living the dream. We used to recite the poem by Langston Hughes that told us to

"Hold fast to dreams,
For if dreams die,
Life is a broken-winged bird
That cannot fly.
Hold fast to dreams,
For if dreams go,
Life is a barren field,
Frozen with snow."

Surely she had held on tightly to her dreams. She had caught the brass ring on the merry-go-round, as one of her little pre-school songs declared that had played and played on its little turntable when she was tiny. She was living out her second chance without dwelling on her past struggles or on any possible future struggles. She looked toward the future with love and light and thanksgiving in her eyes and heart.

Chapter 25 Points of Light

I hope I captured for you, dear reader, how Teresa enjoyed, savored, delighted in the normalcy of her life during those good years, which lasted from the time of her transplant recovery into 2011. Did she have a job as a CEO, travel the world, visit the big cities, go on cruises, experience a movie star life? No, but she did work hard like most Americans, spent many vacation weekends at the beach, traveled to Florida to visit Bradley's brother Martin and his wife, took advantage of local cultural opportunities when possible, went to some great movies, saw everything available on television I think... Once when Bradley went with some guy friends to a car show/race/exhibition she drove herself and Preston to the mountains where Terry and I had rented a cabin and we could listen to the water rushing in the river behind us and chase fireflies in the evening in the backyard. Besides her adventures with Bradley and Preston and the rest of family, she continued to develop new interests through the years - photography, her kitchen window hummingbirds (some of her birds becoming familiar enough that Bradley could hold their feeder in his hands near his face and they would feed there, Teresa snapping pictures as fast as she could), karaoke, and further crafting projects (wreath- and bow-making particularly) which she loved to share with others. She had always loved kaleidoscopes and she was making of her life a colorful combination of those things within her grasp.

Before her transplant Teresa's nutrition had suffered. While she had been a healthy weight in high school, she had experienced some weight gain as a young adult, then lost it before and just after her transplant and during those months of exercise while recovering. She did so love to eat and when she got her appetite back she enjoyed trying out various restaurants again. There were dietary restrictions and while she adhered to many of those, she would tell you she had weaknesses and she did begin to put on weight in those healthy years. Her doctors and nurses would chide her gently. I remember one of her transplant management team nurses, a tiny Korean doll of a woman, picking up a rather small cup from beside Teresa's bed after one of her heart caths, and saying, "In my culture, this is a large portion." Hwajoo loved Teresa and always prodded her toward her healthiest self. Teresa would try from time to time to lose the weight. I tried to cook as low fat and low sugar and low salt as possible when they ate with us, but I think Teresa mostly thought it was "low taste."

I would ask her doctor much later, "Why was it that Teresa seemed healthier when she was carrying all of that extra weight?" He directed this question back to me, "Was she doing well because she was heavy or was she heavy because she was doing well?" Yes, we wish she could have kept the weight off, but it would be the opposite problem that, among other issues, plagued her, us, and every doctor who cared for her eventually. The problems she experienced would eventually result in a weight loss that was puzzling and scary and had us and MUSC scrambling for answers.

It is difficult to wade into that inadequate, turbulent pool of words that are needed to describe the years of 2011 forward. While we did still dance with joy, more and more often the darkness, disguised as various health issues, would tap our shoulders and cut into the waltz. We had to reach up for the strength of our Father in Heaven, reach out to those around us who had strength to share, and reach down to draw each other up at so many places along this bumpy road.

Fling the brush of morning
Against the canvas of the night.
Splatter it with hope and faith
And little spots of light.

We remain thankful for all of the points of light we experienced during the next 3 1/2 years.

PART FOUR

Chapter 26 Mystery Symptoms

In 2011 Teresa began to experience occasional episodes of heartburn, severe continual burping, pain in her chest and back and up to her jaw; her arms even tingled at times and she would get short of breath. Sometimes she could feel her heart pounding, the rate fluctuating, and she might have a "heaviness" in her chest. Having experienced the panic attacks earlier, she and her doctors thought it might be a recurrence or a worsening of those. She would have these episodes and then they would subside, sometimes for weeks before reappearing. The doctors then began to think it could be digestive since she was still regularly taking the meds for anxiety and the heart tests they ordered showed no alarming results. She starting taking Gavascon for reflux and they had her undergo some fairly extensive digestive tests. The endoscopy, colonoscopy, and gallbladder scans, including the HIDA scan, showed no problems to cause what she was feeling.

Teresa had also begun to have problems with her eyes. She had worn contact lenses for a long time and occasionally she would suffer from a scratched cornea. Several years earlier we had had a scare with something they observed in her retina and she had seen a retina specialist. Whatever it was did not turn out to be retinitis pigmentosa, which could have blinded her, but they did observe that the retinas of her eyes were not as they should be. The retina specialist suggested that maybe a virus, perhaps even a virus that could have impacted her heart years ago, had taken a toll in her eyes too. Whatever it was, they thought it had probably been arrested and was not progressing to cause further damage but they wanted to keep track of her eyes nonetheless. (I thought of that from time to time throughout the years. They had told us that her heart disease was hypertrophic cardiomyopathy, maybe idiopathic. We did not pursue the viral cardiomyopathy theory. Whether it was one or the other, it had progressed to dilated cardiomyopathy, which led to the need for the transplant.) All of this explanation and bird walk lead to the statement that anytime Teresa began to have problems with her eyes, our blood ran a little cold. Dr. Mintz at the Columbia Eye Clinic assured us that, while she was not seeing **well**, it appeared to be cornea problems and not the retina trouble progressing. She had a time when she was uncomfortable driving and that hampered her lifestyle somewhat. She soldiered on with her eyeglasses and eye drops, once again doing the very best she could.

I retired that summer from my wonderful career in Lexington School District One. It seemed to be the best time for me to do that. I had given 33 years to education, 28 to school libraries, and my profession was changing some. Our school library was about to be renovated and while I would have loved much about that project, something told me that the energy needed for that might limit what I could do with family, Teresa particularly, and I did not want to lose any time with her. While I had lived with fear, more fear than I should have through the years, her struggle with these new symptoms scared me even more and nudged me to exit at the end of school year 2010-11. It was a bittersweet time of leaving behind a host of good friends and good memories and I knew I would feel an emptiness about that, but I also felt that God was telling me to be open to this new future, whatever it held.

Teresa's symptoms with the heart/panic/digestion (still a question mark as to **what** it was) were worsening by June of 2011, becoming almost unmanageable. She would come near to passing out in some of the episodes she had. We went to MUSC in June with these alarming symptoms and Teresa's tests alarmed them too, the EKG showing what resembled an acute heart attack. They started an echocardiogram, then stopped it when they became fearful and took her to the cath lab. The results were puzzling, because the EKG returned to near-normal. They did say that while the left heart seemed okay, there was some allograft vasculopathy (a thickening and thus narrowing of the coronary vessels) developing in the right side of her heart, a condition that sometimes affects transplant patients. They said it was not a great amount; they were not unduly alarmed by it and it was not anything they could stint. They recommended a pacemaker, telling us that she was experiencing 3rd degree (complete) heart block. In this type of heart block, none of the electrical signals from the atria part of the heart reach the ventricles. On an EKG, the normal heart rate pattern is disrupted.

While she and we dreaded the surgical procedure, we had high hopes for this giving her relief from the distress she was having during these spells and on June 28, 2011 the device was implanted. It was to read for aberrant rate/rhythms and pace accordingly. It did not pace continuously and she was not pacemaker-dependent. It took a while to recover from the surgery, with no heavy lifting, etc. and there were some precautions to observe, with magnets for example, as there had been with her defibrillator years earlier. She was also to have the device periodically checked, which could be done by phone. But overall, once she recovered, she again tried to resume the normalcy of her life, being with family, planning for and showing up at Preston's school and soccer functions, pursuing the hobbies she enjoyed. She did not often know if the device had paced, and actually, it was not pacing much at all in the early months that she had it.

Teresa's symptoms did not subside however. They raged on sporadically throughout the summer months of 2011. She would just try to ride out the episodes she had, which might come on at any time – sometimes she would take the extra Xanax that they had suggested during the attacks (panic?), sometimes extra Tums (digestive?). She might try resting them out, sometimes doing the opposite (staying busy). It did seem that they occurred more often in the evening and during the night than during the day. There seemed to be no one causative factor and no definite, sure-to-work remedy. She might go a week or longer without severe symptoms, but they always returned with a vengeance.

Teresa wanted to work, and her office was flexible in allowing her the hours that she could manage. Since I had retired, I was open to a part-time job and God had one for me. It was in Teresa's office! Jim and Kathy, Rick and Diane, Michelle, Laurie, Darcy, Carolyn, Glenda and other staff welcomed me into a desk in the corner of their office. I was able to be with Teresa some of the week to assist her in the duties she was attempting and I learned so much about the real estate legal field, different from the middle school library but an opportunity to stretch a bit, stay busy, and help Teresa stay busy and have a bit of income. The office staff were wonderful in their support of Teresa through this time. Some days she would come into the office exhausted from being up in the night with what were becoming increasingly worrisome symptoms both physically and emotionally.

In August of 2011 we had to take her in to MUSC's chest pain center (an emergency room of sorts) with symptoms that could no longer be managed. In the ECHO procedure they thought they were observing a heart attack (as had been the scenario in June before she got the pacemaker). They prepared to rush her into the cath lab to see what they could do there when whatever they were observing subsided, again, as it had in June, back to her "normal." They did not go forward with the cath that night, but they did admit Teresa.

The transplant program at MUSC had begun to take on new staff to manage the volume of heart failure and heart transplant patients they were seeing. While Dr. Crumbley and Dr. Van Bakel remained dear to Teresa all throughout the years, she began to be seen by Dr. Michael Craig, Dr. Jennifer Peura, and eventually Dr. Meredith Brisco too, depending on who was on duty when she was in clinic or during admissions. My notes are not clear as to the exact date, but I can see clearly in my memory the visit in Teresa's room by Dr. Craig when he told us that summer what he thought was happening when Teresa had these episodes. These are not his exact words, but his theory was something like, "I think she is having vasospasms. They are fairly rare in transplant patients, but nevertheless, this is what I feel is going on. I want another cath tomorrow to be sure, and there is some medicine that we can give to help this. We also may want to change one of her immunosuppressants to another drug (Rapa) which can make those vessels more flexible." So here was a new word for us, another we had never heard. A coronary artery spasm is a sudden tightening of the muscles inside the arteries of the heart. When it happens, the arteries narrow and keep blood from flowing to the heart. The spasms are brief and temporary but can potentially lead to further heart complications, such as a heart attack. So a new worry in a sense, but also hope that if this was the problem, it could be alleviated or relieved.

One of the young residents had also mentioned to us the word "reinnervation" of the transplanted heart. It seems that at the time of a transplant surgery, the nerves are severed, resulting in "denervation" of the heart. What we understood was that since those nerves do not work as previously, many patients cannot experience pain when cardiac events occur. BUT if a patient's nerves have been reinnervated after transplant it would be possible to experience pain from such events. Perhaps this is why it had been assumed that Teresa's symptoms were panic or digestive, not cardiac, but we and the doctors would come to realize that summer of 2011 that what she had been experiencing **was** coming from her heart, maybe exacerbated by some degree of panic attacks and digestive discomfort at times. When they did her cath on that August afternoon in 2011, the vasospasm did show up – that contracting of the coronary artery. Dr. Powers reiterated to us that these did not often show up in transplant patients. It pains me even now as I think how she had struggled all those nights with what must have felt like a heart attack every time. It seems clear to me that her heart was one that had experienced at least a partial reinnervation.

They did make the decision to change Teresa's immunosuppressants from Cellcept and Neoral to Everolimus and Prograf. It was hoped that these might help some with the allograft vasculopathy that was starting to show up in their testing. They also added Norvasc and Imdur for vasospasms. They said these would help to relax the vessels that were spasming. They told us that about 10% of patients had swelling in their legs and ankles when they took one of these two medicines. She was one of those unfortunate 10%. Once again, she adjusted. When the weather was cold, she wore compression socks. Since everyone was wearing socks at that time, she did not feel that she was "fashion compromised." But when the weather got warmer (and our South Carolina summers are not described as just warm, but some years as almost an inferno), she had to devise other options. She WOULD wear flip-flops, her favorite, with her toes always painted up in some bright color. She kept her feet elevated at every opportunity, which helped, so that she could walk some without extreme pressure in her feet and legs. If she stayed on her feet too long, though, it would take longer for them to get back to normal. Mornings were best – they had rested all night.

We would both continue to work at Jim Sketo's office. It was like a family there and they just worked around her doctors' appointments, hospital admissions, "can't do it today" days. Overall, with the adjustment for the new medicines, she carried on as normally as possible for herself, Bradley, and Preston. She continued to make sure Preston was in order for school, soccer, church, etc. and she **always** made certain he had a big birthday. They liked to take him to Myrtle Beach around the time of his birthday. The rates were lower, they had trick-or-treating at Broadway at the Beach, and he loved the indoor water recreation there. In October of 2011 they planned their trip and were able to get there. She called us from there though to tell us, "I am so tired and short of breath that I can barely make it even a little ways before having to sit down. I seem to be coughing all the time with some kind of respiratory thing." She had given in to staying in the room for spells and letting her fellows get out to have whatever fun they could.

Everything that happened like this always sent me into high alert. Obviously I always assumed it was her heart and many times that was either directly or indirectly the case. When she got back to town and continued with that fatigue, I insisted she see Dr. Martin locally. Her hemoglobin was extremely low and while she had had low hemoglobin before, these numbers came back alarmingly low. Dr. Martin began to treat that and he also gave some antibiotics in case her coughing was a bacterial infection instead of viral. Slowly she rallied back from that scary period to enjoy a rocky but fairly normal end to 2011. Christmas always seemed to revitalize her no matter her worries about physical health and she was determined to enjoy that.

Chapter 27 Scariest Morning Yet

By 2012, despite Imdur, Norvasc, and Metoprolol, Teresa continued with the vasospasm spells. Each time she got to an unmanageable place, the docs would increase the dosages. It would help for a time but always returned. The year progressed into summer. I don't remember any further extremely alarming news from the heart cath she had in June of that year. It mostly revealed what we already knew – that there was some allograft vasculopathy and yes, it was vasospasms she was experiencing. Her pacemaker seemed to be performing okay in the checks that were periodically made.

On the evening of July 17th Teresa experienced extreme symptoms with the vasospasms again. She said that her chest felt heavy and her arms tired. She said that she felt that her body was "rocking." When she called MUSC they said to go to a local hospital to be checked. Sometimes they ordered her pacemaker to be checked over the landline phone and if it alarmed them, they would send her in locally to be sure all was okay. On this night they told her to go in to a local emergency room. She and Bradley came to our house first and she was so very distressed, yet fatigued too, that we called an ambulance and had her transported to Palmetto Richland. When the doctors in the ER there checked her out, they called MUSC. MUSC's physicians asked that they do nothing to Teresa except get her to them as soon as possible. There was no medical transport available until morning. There **was** a helicopter available but they did not believe it to be an emergency of such a dire nature and planned to move her by ambulance as soon as possible on the morning of the 18th. We had a mostly wakeful night at the ER all of that night. They monitored her and drew blood, but did not actually know what the matter was.

I was the one who could go with Teresa most readily that next morning. Bradley had begun working at Southeastern Freight Lines, which was wonderful throughout Teresa's illness (excellent health insurance coverage, understanding superiors and coworkers, etc.) but he was in a proving period and had not yet built up a great deal of leave time. Since the doctors, while taking this very seriously, did not consider it a life-threatening emergency, it was decided that I would go and let our family in Lexington know in frequent updates by phone and texts how everything was going. None of us could have imagined what the next few hours and days were going to hold.

There was a special ambulance that came on duty fairly early on the morning of July 18th. As I recall it was described as a kind of emergency room on wheels. The driver and I would sit up front and Teresa and several EMT's would be in back. I remember starting out – the driver was very courteous and calm and professional – and the first thing he did was speak the trip's mission into his recording device with something that resembled: "Leaving Palmetto Richland at (whatever the exact time was) o'clock with 36-year-old female non-emergency cardiac patient... destination Medical University of South Carolina in Charleston." This gentleman was intent on his job, which was to get us all safely there as quickly as he could. We were running no lights or siren but not wasting time in the early minutes of our trip. He would correspond with the medics in the back from time to time but I could only hear his side of the conversation. Everything appeared stable during these first several miles. Along about Orangeburg one of the EMT's came forward in the ambulance to address me. Just as my world had turned on a doctor's words on August 11, 1987 in his diagnosis, it lurched again when she said to me, "Mrs. Edwards, Teresa dropped out on us. We thought we would be pulling in to the Orangeburg Regional Hospital for help, but we have resuscitated her and we are now going to turn the lights and siren on this ambulance to do our best to get her to MUSC."

Why I did not become hysterical at this point (that would come a little later in the morning!) I really don't know. For one thing, I knew that that would not help Teresa. I could not hear a thing of what was going on back there, so she probably could not hear us up front, but I felt I needed to be calm. I also remembered my friend Penny's advice: "When you can't even pray, just tell God, "Lord, I need your help. Lord, I need your help." That is what I did. A numbing calm settled on me, even as the driver picked up his pace. This man expected the cars ahead of him to move over and he drove as though to convey that expectation to every driver on the road. There were no exceptions – as we bore down on traffic in our lane, each vehicle made a way for us. I did not know if Teresa was still with us as we approached MUSC, but when we arrived, she was still as well as when they had revived her. The driver pulled to the door that he had been instructed to approach for quickest access to ICU and they wheeled her in. I followed. No sooner had they wheeled her into the glassed-in room of Intensive Care, I heard a nurse shout, "Get James. She's seizing!" Dr. James Hadstate was the doctor, a "Fellow" (physician who has completed a residency and is pursuing further training in a specialty) who was on duty. Dr. Van Bakel was also on the floor at this moment, and I looked up to see him racing, literally, toward the room. Teresa was in cardiac arrest again.

I was outside this room as they worked on her. While I knew she probably was not conscious, I could not bear to think that she felt alone. I knew I could not go there, but reason left me and I began to call, "Teresa, I'm here. Mama's here. I'm right here, Teresa. Just outside!" I felt the kindest arms encircle me and I don't know which of the staff it was, but I heard her say, "Why don't we walk around to the chapel? Would that work?" I thought it would. I was getting prepared to lose Teresa that day, and I wanted to be as close to God as I could get if that was going to happen. When I got to the chapel, I fell on my face and begged. As I contemplated the events of the last hour or so, I felt a bit as I had when she suffered that stroke in 1996: "**How** will she get over this? **Will** she get over this? How will we bear losing her this day?" God forgive me, but I fully expected the worst.

A chaplain came to me and we both prayed. The EMTs from the ambulance came by and spoke to me on their way out. I remember thanking them and telling them that as long as I had a memory, I would not forget them. Then one of the attending doctors came. When he said that they needed to do a heart cath, I could not believe my ears. First of all, Teresa was still here, praise God. Secondly, there must be some hope for her. Then mixed with those thoughts was my fear that she could not endure the cath because of what had occurred. There was obviously no choice, though, so they prepared to proceed. I called Terry and Bradley with the news of what had occurred and they immediately began to make their way to Charleston.

Teresa had been revived during those early moments in the ICU and intubated and vented. When we saw her after the cath, there were, as after transplant, all sorts of tubes and lines coming out of her. Once again, we knew we were observing a miracle, but we were still scared to death. The doctors could not definitively determine the cause for the arrests. They spoke of the vasospasms perhaps "trenching down" into her heart rhythm, a medical term or some kind of jargon which I had not heard before, but the fact remained that this was just their speculation at this juncture. The focus would be on observing her during the initial hours and days after these events, keeping her from arresting again if possible, then make a plan for it not reoccurring. That first night in ICU was a traumatic one, but she had a wonderful nurse who moved around the big and small medical devices in the room like an angel, calm and efficient. If any slight variation in what was supposed to be happening occurred, she was in high alert and would spring into action but not in an alarming way. She knew to the letter about the dosages of medicine going into Teresa and she knew what to adjust up or down as various symptoms happened. She was vigilant! I don't know her name and I don't believe we ever saw her again after this admission, but I do not forget her and the professionalism and acute caution she displayed that night.

While Teresa was there in ICU she had at least one other "near miss" when they called the crash cart, but she came around on her own without them having to use it. She continued to have spasms and pacing in the nights, though, along with burning in her back, chest, arms, and jaw. It came in waves. The doctors were still puzzled. They were beginning to look at the time sequence and trying to determine which came first: the burning/chest pain or the pacemaker beginning to pace. In subsequent days they began to call in other specialists to see if there was some other condition that could be causing these problems. They consulted a rheumatologist, checked on the adrenal gland, hormones, blood vessel performance, even ordering an abdominal CT scan and urine studies. Her blood pressure was trending low. She knew that her pacemaker was pacing much more now than it had earlier – she could feel it. It seemed to be working correctly when they checked its performance, but they did adjust some things about it. Teresa had been taking Norvasc, Imdur, and Metoprolol to help with the vasospasms. They increased her Metoprolol a bit and wanted to try the drug Diltiazem in hopes of preventing the spasms. Their theory was that if the Diltiazem worked, it was probably spasms. By July 28 they were guardedly optimistic that they had found the "cocktail" that worked best for the spasms.

I recall Teresa's friend Becky Scott coming to Charleston one evening during this scary scary time to be with us. Her calming presence was a comfort that I never forget. Her husband Bobby took care of the home front in Columbia as she drove herself to us and gave away her compassion and strength so generously as we struggled. While we all knew how serious Teresa's issues were, it helped her to talk about usual things, and this is what Becky did as she sat with her. It delighted Teresa, really, and helped her see the life to which she wanted to rebound more clearly. I fretted that Becky had the late dark night as her companion on her return trip to Columbia and was glad to know when she had made it back safely. I am thankful that Becky remains in my life and heart along with her sweet family.

I remember how much Teresa wanted to leave the hospital from this traumatic visit. By July 29 she was swelling with fluid and they had to give her diuretics to get some of it off. They worked with that for the next several days, and while she improved enough to go home, there was still some fluid in her tissues and in her lungs when she prepared to leave on August 2. She was to take the diuretics they were prescribing and have labs drawn locally to check indicators of kidney/other progress. They wanted her weight to go down to what it had been when she had been admitted – the excess fluid was not good.

Allison, one of the transplant nurses, was sitting with us for a while on the day of discharge. As wonderful as she was, I think she hardly knew what to say in light of the ordeal Teresa had just come through. There were still uncertainties in the cause/diagnosis of what had occurred and in the treatment plan, too, really. Teresa was visibly worried and scared and not talking about it. I was worried and scared and trying not to show it. What I remember saying to that nurse and Teresa that day was, "We are going to march bravely into our future." Two truths which I often repeat even now in various situations came to me as I said those words right out into the midst of our fears: (1) Not one person alive, despite good health and good fortune, knows what the day holds, and (2) God did, does, and always will have a plan for every one of us.

Chapter 28 Financial Decision

As we had lingered in the hospital during this time, one other thing became crystal clear to me. Maybe I need to say right here that hardly anything decision-wise in this journey was ever **absolutely** clear to me. Every medical decision we made I agonized over. Is this really the recommended route or the correct diagnosis? Should I question the doctors more? Should we insist on another opinion? Should we do this test or that procedure sooner or wait until later? Is this **really** what God wants us to do? I second-guessed too much, and it was not just medical issues, but insurance matters and financial decisions. Maybe it was the devil in the mix. And yet even as I ponder this, and as contradictory as it might sound, I believe we gave the best we could at any given moment. The decision that came clearly to me in July of 2012 was to apply for Teresa's social security disability benefits.

I thought back to when she was disabled before transplant and what a harrowing process it was. We went through several denials, not obtaining benefits for her until she had that stroke. I was prepared for similar delays, having heard many say, "Almost everyone is denied the first time – just count on it." Should I get a lawyer? I had finally done that before and did not feel that it had expedited the process so much. I decided to go it alone in the first attempt this time and when I began to compile the conditions Teresa was experiencing, a great sadness visited me. She wanted so much to be well, to take care of Bradley and Preston, to work like a healthy person. Hopefully if she recovered well she could still do some meaningful work even if she received benefits - there was provision in the law for that. But I knew, beyond any doubt, that it was right to try to get something for her each month. She had enjoyed her time in the workforce in healthier times and even when she began to struggle she continued to work, many days when she may have needed to be at home.

I perused the Social Security disability application and began to compose. Among the medical data to be listed were

Conditions: Complications of heart transplant received 12 years earlier, including vasospasms, cardiac insufficiency, swelling/weight gain, shortness of breath, pounding heart, chest pain and heaviness in chest, fatigue/lack of energy, coughing, elevated creatinine (kidney function decreasing), pacemaker performance, low blood pressure, cardiac arrest. Also added to this list were: digestive concerns (burping, acid reflux, heartburn, past bouts with ulcerative colitis), anemia, anxiety and depression, and vision problems (inflammation of cornea, also periodic check of retinas).

Medical tests performed: Cardiac catheterization, echo cardiograms, EKGs, countless blood tests, urine studies, pacemaker evaluations, abdominal CT scan, pelvic ultrasound, CT scan of kidneys, chest X-rays, eye exams....

Medicines: By prescription, Cellcept, Prednisone, Cyclosporine, Imdur, Diltiazem, Norvasc, Pravastatin, Xanax, Welbutrin, Nexium, Bumex, Nitroglycerin, Ferrous Sulfate, and eye drops for inflammation, as well as a number of supplements like Potassium Chloride, Magnesium Oxide, Calcium Citrate, then Aspirin as a means for keeping stroke risk minimal...

There were sections to fill out about education, job description, physical strength, endurance, insurance, and consent to release records and contact doctors. Nothing I wrote, with Teresa's input, was exaggerated in any way. It was just the awful truth.

We finalized the application in early August. While the Social Security Administration did write to Teresa to request that she sign an electronic medical records release form and to ask that she provide proof of earnings, there was no other glitch in the granting of her benefits based on this first application we submitted – no appeals necessary. While I was thankful and overjoyed that she was granted her benefits so quickly, my joy was tempered by the sad fact that she was, indeed, very sick, as even the SSA was acknowledging.

Chapter 29 More Surgery

Meanwhile, even as the Social Security application was progressing, we traveled homeward on August 2 after the "cardiac arrest hospital stay" as we started to refer to it. On August 8 we took Teresa back to MUSC with swelling all over her body, it seemed. Her creatinine was creeping up. (You will continue to read the word "creatinine" herein, because Teresa's kidney function would become a constant concern for all the weeks, months, and years that she lived.) They admitted her again and gave her intravenous diuretics. She stayed about a week. She fretted over the time she had to be away from Preston in these hospital visits. Bradley's mother was steadfast in caring for him while Teresa and I and sometimes Bradley too were in Charleston, but Teresa missed him and he missed her and the normalcy of their home routine. When they discharged her, she knew that she was due back for a clinic visit in two weeks. Sometimes I think she tried to minimize her symptoms to the docs at times so that she could avoid a hospital admission and be at home with her boys.

During the next clinic visit on August 30 there was no disguising her symptoms, though. She was coughing frequently, was short of breath, trembling, allergic (her eyes particularly), and doing that same burping that she had been doing all along. Also, since the cardiac arrest, the blood vessel in the right side of Teresa's neck had been visibly pulsating. Dr. Crumbley noted that there was fluid in her abdomen and there was fluid in or around the right lower lobe of her lung. A chest x-ray revealed this lung fluid to be a "pleural effusion" and it was another diagnosis that would continue to haunt us. The questions that began to arise as they noted her increase in swelling were, "What is it from? Is it right-sided heart failure (from the cardiac arrest, maybe?) or from a leaking tricuspid valve (also new since the cardiac arrest)?" They were going to ponder and discuss the possibilities for cause and treatment, but meanwhile, they gave her a cocktail of diuretics for the accumulated fluid and let her go home, instructing her to return in a week for another clinic visit. They hoped at that time to see a marked reduction in the fluid retention.

The September 5 lab work in clinic revealed a further decrease in kidney function, probably due to the strong combination of diuretics. Her creatinine number had gone up even further but the lung was not yet open either – neither of which was good news. Dr. Crumbley, who saw her in clinic, was visibly alarmed. They admitted her.

Still attempting to determine the cause of the fluid retention, they did a right heart cath early in this admission. We were told right after that the cath showed nothing significant, that it looked good. Maybe they described the results this way in light of all that her heart had been through. They also did a thoracentesis early on and pulled a liter of fluid from Teresa's chest. On September 8 when Dr. Craig came in, he made several observations: "The swelling in your legs is probably the meds we have you on. Continue to use the compression socks. The fluid in your lungs is probably **not** the meds, but we are not sure what it is. The numbers from the cath are pretty good – the right side pressures are a little high, but not exceedingly high. So why is the tricuspid valve leaky? Is the right heart a bit stiff, maybe from the cardiac arrest? Or could the pacemaker wires, which typically feed through the tricuspid valve, be keeping the valve from closing properly?" These were questions the team would consider. He said they were on a search for the missing piece.

By September 11, the creatinine level was coming down, but slowly. Dr. Craig reported that, according to the tests, there did not appear to be heart damage below the valve. He thought the pacemaker leads might be problematic and suggested that they be repositioned to bypass the tricuspid valve, through which they were presently passing, and be attached to the heart muscle itself. If this did not work, there was another surgery that involved tightening the ring of the tricuspid valve with some sort of wire, a more involved surgery. They were leaning toward the repositioning of the pacemaker leads, which did not sound like too complicated a process.

On September 12 Dr. Craig was still rounding. With creatinine not good but still slowly decreasing, indicating that her kidneys were somewhat better, the team made the decision to go ahead and recommend the repositioning of the pacemaker leads. They wanted to reduce her Norvasc to 10 instead of 15 and give her the Imdur at night instead of in the morning. Teresa was opposed to this. I had questions about her kidneys, about the initial reports from the heart cath, and certainly about the upcoming surgery. Dr. Craig seemed to think that the high Norvasc dose had not been good for the kidneys and as for the initial report that the heart cath "looked good" and showed "nothing significant" he was less clear but seemed adamant that the repositioning of the leads should give a chance at relief of some of the fluid problem. Her main symptom on September 12 was that neck vessel jumping. They did want to adjust her cyclosporine dose because of her kidneys. They told us at this point that they were working to achieve balance between the kidneys and heart – to get the optimum from both without further damage to either.

We saw two doctors later in the day on September 12. Dr. Toole, the surgeon, and later a Dr. Thompson came in to visit. They needed to explain the surgery and its risks. We were told that it was not "textbook." They had done this kind of surgery before, but not on a transplant patient. They sounded confident, though, and told us what to typically expect: they would go in either through her transplant incision or through her ribs under her arm. She would be in surgery 2-5 hours, perhaps spend some time in ICU, have a recovery of 2-3 days in the hospital, a drain tube ... It did not sound as simple as first presented but Teresa was willing to try this in hopes of feeling better on a more permanent basis.

On September 13 they reattached the leads, using an opening in her ribs. The doctors said they would know more about how much it had helped things in an ECHO the next day. They would also check her pacemaker. As it turned out, they could not do the ECHO right away because she had extreme pain. They were working on managing that and getting her to where she could move more. She also had trouble voiding and that was alarming due to the already diminished kidney function. Her creatinine had come down a tiny bit more, but they told her she would not go home before Tuesday or Wednesday.

Teresa's creatinine level had not decreased further by September 18 (six days after the surgery) but since everything else was mostly stable, Doctor Craig was going to let her go back to Lexington. The valve, he said, was still leaky, but less leaky he hoped. He said they might see further improvement over the next several weeks to one month. He said tightening the valve in that other, more complex surgery was not out of the question. They would do an ECHO in another month.

A few days after Teresa was dismissed from the hospital she did not seem to have as much coughing or burping, but she did still have pain which she was controlling with the meds, while being concerned about still needing them. She began to have a loss of appetite, some nausea, and she could feel her heart pounding and "jumping around" as she described it. We took her to the MUSC chest pain center for a pacemaker check, which seemed to indicate that the pacemaker was performing okay.

We went back to clinic on September 25 and her labs at that visit showed a high potassium level and elevated creatinine again. She felt achy and was not sleeping well and the rounds with the burping, coughing, and heartburn had returned. Dr. Crumbley read the discharge report. He was happy to see that the EF (ejection fraction) of her heart was adequate, but he was not happy about her kidney function. They still wanted to reduce the Norvasc dose to try to give her higher blood pressure and she was still opposed to this because she feared those vasospasms so dreadfully, but he explained some things about the half-life of the drug and she always trusted what Dr. Crumbley said.

The MUSC staff really seemed to want Teresa to feel better but this surgery was obviously taking more recovery than even they had anticipated. They adjusted medicines and she adjusted once again to a "new normal" life with the diminishing kidney function, low blood pressure because of the vasospasm drugs, and some diminished stamina from all of it. She set her mind toward getting as well as she could from all of these events of the summer of 2012. She had blood drawn locally fairly frequently during September, October, and November and MUSC corresponded with her about results, making adjustments as necessary. Not only were there adjustments in medicines but sometimes there were changes to the times that she could take them because of their interactions with each other or their ineffectiveness if taken too close together.

The next clinic visit I have in my notes is the one on December 13 of that year. She had lost weight, her creatinine was down to 1.6 and those were great strides. She seemed to have recovered from the surgery as much as she was going to but the leaky tricuspid valve had not shown much improvement. Her neck vessel still jumped and her chest was never totally clear of fluid after the events of that summer. But Christmas was coming and that always lit a spark in our girl. She had always planned and organized from whatever energy plane she was on to enjoy her favorite holiday of the year, and while she could not physically decorate as much as prior, she did all she could and then directed others who loved her as to what still needed doing! She placed in her calendar all of the Taylor, Edwards, and Power events so that she and her family would not miss a single one.

Chapter 30 2013

Teresa wanted to do what work she could for the office and Jim allowed her to work from her home computer on some things. When she could go into the office, she did, and I was still there at the office as well to help out on a part-time basis. Teresa was still proficient with those right-of-way projects, consulting with her boss by phone for clarification when needed, directing me in some of the computer data entry that preceded and followed them. I could also make the copies she needed and do some of the footwork that she could not do.

The office staff remained understanding about the times Teresa had to be out for planned as well as unexpected doctors' visits. Ever since the cardiac arrest that prior summer, we had stopped with most local medical treatment and for almost everything that came up we went straight to MUSC, knowing that there was where she would most likely end up. She did still see Dr. Martin at the Lexington Family Practice occasionally and she saw Dr. Mintz at the Columbia Eye Clinic for her eye problems which were ongoing. When she needed labs drawn, which was fairly often, that could be done locally too at the lab that could produce the fastest results and that was in her insurance's network.

The doctors continued to try to achieve a balance between heart function and kidney function. Blood pressure that was too low was not good for kidney effusion. If too high, that could contribute to vasospasms. Neither was a good scenario. They wanted her checking in regularly at the heart clinic at MUSC as well as getting labs drawn and having her pacemaker checked by phone on a regular basis. Teresa's clinic visit in March showed that she had lost about 35 pounds since the late summer and her blood pressure was low but not alarmingly so. Her creatinine was down to 1.5 which was good compared to prior visits. The blood vessel in her neck was still pulsing at about the same level as it had since the cardiac arrest.

During the spring and summer of 2013 Teresa had a young man named Jake Paul on her mind and heart. Jake was a local high school student in the school where Teresa's cousin Ann was guidance counselor and Ann had let Teresa know about him. Jake had developed a cardiomyopathy in 2012 which led to his need for a transplant. Teresa wanted to offer her support and encouragement to Jake and his family and she corresponded with his mom some and she and I went to see him one day at MUSC when his dad was there with him. Jake was struggling. This was a young man who loved the outdoors and he had a passion for fishing especially. His heart failure became so severe that he had had an LVAD (Left Ventricular Assist Device) implanted to bridge him over to transplant. He did get a new heart in November 2013 and Teresa followed his case closely.

Teresa continued to have problems with her eyes during this summer. They would get a little better then become blurry again. She had a scratched cornea which did not respond to drops. She had to resort to wearing her glasses, which she did not like, but there was no other solution. When wearing those contacts she experienced burning, itching, and looked as if she had been crying and she was **never** a crybaby. She had earlier on developed a reading habit for Christian fiction and she was pretty dependent on her technology devices too, as well as wanting to work for Lexington Title, so she needed to be able to see. When she realized how serious the problem with her vision had become, she gave in to getting a new pair of glasses. Preston helped her pick these out and they were plenty glitzy.

Teresa always presented her ultimate fashionable self when she went to her MUSC appointments. Some of the staff usually noticed. Even Dr. Crumbley, who Teresa always loved through good and bad times, commented on how "sparkly" she always was. Once during a clinic visit he turned to me (being about the same age as he) and asked if I remembered Dick Tracy. I said I did but that was not one of the comic strips I had regularly read. He was recalling the character "Sparkle Plenty" and the more he thought about it and observed Teresa's big rings, glittery glasses, etc. he just had to see if he was remembering the name correctly. Next thing we knew he was googling there in the exam room for Dick Tracy and after a few minutes he turned and said, "Yep, that's what I can call you now. Sparkle Plenty." He made us laugh, as he often did.

Teresa's little Zack was having health issues during 2013 too. He had developed arthritis and he could not breathe very well at times. He had been such a source of joy to Teresa and he had spent much of his life in her lap and on her bed. When he could no longer jump up and down so well they put a "beddy," as Teresa called it, beside her recliner so that he could be at least that near to her. She knew the time was coming to let him go but it was a hard hard decision for her to make. She finally made the phone call for that last appointment, which was to be late in the afternoon after her work and Bradley's. She got together a last good meal that he could eat and served it to him the night before. She made him comfortable in his bed, which was in their laundry room while they were away. She turned his radio on. When she got in from town that appointed day, he had laid his little head down on his own bed and died. Teresa and Bradley buried him at the edge of their yard and his grave is still marked by some of the things she put there. It was a time of great sadness for her and for all of us because he had been a part of the family for their entire married life. He was a spirited little fellow who brought spark, energy, and mischief to the house. Teresa later said, "I should have cremated Zack so that he could be inside with me." My brother William, who, along with his fiancé Cheryl was a prayer warrior for us throughout our journey, reminded us, as we discussed the issue of animals going to heaven, "The Lord can give you anything he wants you to have in heaven." I never forget this. Pet lovers, I have a cocker spaniel that I am going to ask God for when I get there. I feel like Zack is that one for Teresa. Chloe the cat that Teresa and Bradley rescued from the parking lot at the pancake restaurant will probably make it there too!

Chapter 31 Surgery Yet Again

On June 11 Teresa was scheduled for the yearly heart cath. It showed some disease in the arteries and the pressures a little abnormal but not unduly alarming for what she had been through. She was still coughing, swelling, and her creatinine had risen slightly. Dr. Crumbley thought that there was fluid in her chest still and that her liver was also big. On June 18 Dr. Craig made rounds in clinic and he said they were still pondering her swelling/fluid issue. He said another possibility when fluid collects is that there is some smoldering rejection going on with the heart. Teresa asked about a re-transplant if the time came. He said he thought they would certainly consider that. While there was some allograft vasculopathy, as they had been telling her for a time, and these other problems as well, they wanted to stave off a second transplant for as long as possible.

On June 27 Teresa had lost ten more pounds, this since two weeks prior. Her creatinine had crept up a bit more. When asked about her energy level by Dr. Peura at this visit, she said, "Yes, I have SOME energy." When asked if she was having breathing problems, she responded, "No, not right now." I think this was one of those times that Teresa just wanted to be able to go back home and do what she was able to do, so she may not have totally offered up all of her symptoms too freely. She rocked along with all she could do with the decreased kidney function and the fluid retention as well as the episodes of vasospasms and pacemaker activity.

My notes show labs drawn about once a week in August and sporadically in September and October to check for kidney function, potassium and other levels. She had at least one chest x-ray to see about the pleural effusion and how much it was increasing. The docs agreed that the fluid in her chest was a separate issue from the swelling in her legs. In October she experienced her heart racing, feeling like jelly in her chest, and feeling especially hard heart beats. They admitted her to explore what was causing these symptoms as well as the fluid in her chest.

In the middle of one night during this hospital stay the telemetry alarm went off on her screen and they came in to do an EKG. Upon examining her EKGs and questioning Teresa and Bradley further (and Bradley pushed them for further investigation because he knew these recent developments were new) they determined that there were PACs coming from the top of her heart and PVCs coming from the bottom and the pacemaker was not "seeing" all of the P-waves and they needed to adjust it for that. As I recall, they described it as adjusting the "sensitivity floor" of the device.

Other tests and procedures during that October admission were more chest x-rays, kidney checks, and a thoracentesis to draw fluid from around her lung that they thought was possibly compromising her breathing and certainly was causing some of the coughing. Throughout the fall they continued to puzzle over the fluid retention in her chest. There really did not seem to be enough of a tricuspid valve leak to attribute it to that. There did not seem to be enough heart failure to take the blame. Her kidneys were not performing optimally by any means, but the diuretic cocktail (i.e. varying doses of Bumex and Metolozone occasionally too) was helping them along and they did not think her kidneys were totally to blame. They began to think that maybe it was a combination of things. Meanwhile, her chest continued to take on fluid. They added some Coreg to her regimen of drugs and her blood pressure trended even lower.

There was a hospital admission in early December. The cardiologists were consulting pulmonary specialists by then. They needed to know the source and the kind of fluid that was collecting. Various doctors would come in and talk aloud about various possibilities: "That neck vessel is pulsating so there **is** the tricuspid valve still leaking. But that does not usually yield such a rapid accumulation of fluid." "There **could** be an infection." "It's **possible** there is some scar tissue on the lung." "There is obviously some rather high pressure in the blood vessels forcing water out..." "The pressure in the left side of the heart is a bit high but that is fairly normal for an older transplanted heart." "What if there is some constrictive pericardial disease – the pericardium (lining around the heart) might have hardened." "Then there could be diastolic heart failure..." Nobody could settle on a definitive answer. They seemed to all be genuinely puzzled, desiring an answer, and at a loss to find it.

Dr. Huggins, one of the pulmonary doctors, wanted to test the fluid in the thoracentesis that was done during this admission (2.5 liters was drawn off and Teresa lost a number of pounds as a result), and when he did, he described it as a chylous effusion, which Wikipedia defines as resulting from "lymph formed in the digestive system called chyle accumulating in the pleural cavity due to either disruption or obstruction of the thoracic duct from a leaking thoracic duct system." She was weighing about 128 pounds, more or less, in December, depending on how much fluid she was holding. This was a tremendous weight loss for her from even a year prior and they were beginning to worry about it and we were too. They put her on the diet recommended for chylothorax and while the fluid did change color to indicate that there was less chyle (lymph and emulsified fats) in it, it continued to form and the thoracenteses had to continue to get it out of her chest. These procedures gave her some relief but in a few short weeks it would be necessary to have it done again. Draining the fluid caused a nutritional loss which was not good for her overall health. They were starting to infuse protein after every drain. My notes indicate that on December 2, 9, 19, and 30 she had this process repeated (two of those during her hospital stay early in the month). There was always a chance that a lung could be punctured, an infection develop, etc. When it became obvious that this (thoracentesis) process was going to need to continue, they began to think toward other solutions. Dr. Denlinger, the lung surgeon, was brought in to advise, and he and Dr. Huggins and Dr. Crumbley began to consult.

I never did get the impression that the cardiologists were absolutely convinced that this was the very best solution, but they finally agreed (based on Pulmonary's assessment and assurance that "This is the plan!") to propose a thoracic duct ligation. What this entailed was a chest surgery that would stop the leakage, wherever it was (and they were not sure exactly where it was) along the thoracic duct system. While the fluid would not back up in her chest, it would go to her abdomen temporarily they said. Dr. Huggins said that the fluid would be mostly a cosmetic issue and in time, the fluid would find its "venous channels" and she would not have it in her abdomen anymore either. He did caution that this would take time – in some patients several months or even longer. One female patient he recalled took two years for this to happen (and it occurred suddenly) but he considered it extreme for it to have taken this long. Six months was usually the outer window from what we could surmise.

Teresa was getting weary of the shortness of breath, the repeated fluid pulls from her chest, and the inability to do very much at all, so when Dr. Denlinger and Dr. Huggins suggested the procedure, her response was, "Sign me up!" - another example of bravely reaching for solutions despite the pitfalls and risks of yet another surgery. They did not think it would be too involved and wanted to schedule the surgery for early in 2014. Teresa wanted so fiercely to be as well as possible and we of course wanted that for her too. Sending the chest fluid to her belly concerned me some, especially considering that her feet and legs still swelled from the heart spasm drugs, but the reassurance that it would subside carried us forward.

Along with, or shortly after, the thoracic duct ligation they also were considering another possible procedure: a talc pleurodesis which entailed inserting into the chest a "talc" of sorts that would adhere the outer surface of the lung to the membrane surrounding that lung. Their hope was that they could stop much of the fluid from collecting within the pleura (lung membrane) with the surgical ligation of the duct and then seal the lung space there with the talc to keep it from refilling. We were learning once again of medical conditions and procedures that we had never heard of before.

On January 3 they did ligate the thoracic duct. The surgery lasted 2 hours and 45 minutes. She was on the lung floor and was in a great deal of pain. We were encouraged when there was very low fluid output from the chest tubes at first, but by Jan. 7 it had picked up in output. They left the chest tube in. Teresa's blood pressure was low and they came in during the night to do an EKG based on a monitor reading that had alarmed them. The next morning, January 8, Dr. Denlinger came by, the pulmonary fellows came by, and Dr. Craig was the cardiologist who was rounding. The fluid was changing color by now – back to the cloudy version. They thought it would be best to perform that talc pleurodesis procedure and Dr. Denlinger's physician's assistant came in to do that about 6:15.

By the next day, the outflow of chest fluid had diminished and we were so glad, so encouraged. Teresa's bowels and bladder were slower to "wake up" with each surgery she had, though, and until these functions improved she would not be discharged. What we had thought might be a couple of days inpatient once again stretched into a prolonged stay of ten days. She was discharged around the 12th of January.

PART FIVE

Chapter 32 Toughest Lap Begins

Probably more than any other time in our journey, I am troubled by the eight months of suffering that Teresa endured beginning early in 2014. No doubt, it is the hardest part of her story to write. Was it because we had such high hopes for this (major for her) surgery that she undertook in her quest for better health? Was it a disappointment in the (failure of the) suggestion and assurance we received that this was "the fix?" Was it an anger with ourselves that we did not push for other solutions before we embarked on the path we did?

Even now, four years later, I wonder sometimes if it could have been different. We know that she could not have continued with the fluid in her chest. Surely that much is clear. Treatments for what she was experiencing were limited, but I sometimes think, "What if the octreotide drug had been started earlier?" (This was attempted later in the battle.) What if they had tried a pleuroperitoneal shunt or external drain through placement of a catheter system? (This I found in some later research, but it sounds awful too and probably would not have been an option because of the size the shunt would have needed to be for the kind of fluid causing her problem.) I am also troubled by the cause of the lymphatic leak: why this chylothorax to begin with? We read that it is sometimes caused by trauma to the chest from surgery or other events. She had had to be revived by CPR in that ambulance in July 2012 (but she **was** revived, we reminded ourselves!) and she had had that pacemaker lead replaced in surgery in September of that year. Did something go awry in either event? These are among the questions I referred to in this book's introduction.

What if and what if and what if? But because I know that God has a plan, I cling to the belief that He led us to do the best that we saw to do in any given moment, in every given situation. I want to believe this about our MUSC doctors as well. Maybe things could have been even worse than they seemed to be for the next seven+ months after that January 2014 surgery. I find myself writing in shorter and shorter sessions as I try to describe our warrior, as the words in my notes, in my memory, and in my heart are painful ones. Not to forget, though, from earlier in the journey: Count it all joy.

I had a teacher friend who lost her husband to ALS in 2004. I bought a journal for her as she cared for him and wrote inside, "Sometimes God shows us, in the truth of our own words, the way he wants us to go." And I amend that now to include the way he wants **others** to go too if our journey can help someone. It is necessary to truthfully spill ourselves out to God (He knows our darkest thoughts and deepest fears anyway) and also when the timing is right, to family, trusted friends, acquaintances, even strangers that He puts in our path. I also know, though, that sometimes we need to be silent, to contemplate, to meditate, to keep some things until the time becomes right, if ever, to share. Where did I hear it, "In the silence, a rumble of the truth?" All of this rambling is to say that my own journaling advice failed me sometimes during these darkest of days. I also know though that God never did. I saw in one of the lab rooms at MUSC at some visit during the years a small sign that read,

"Man said to God, 'WHERE ARE YOU?'

God said to man, 'RIGHT HERE. Where are YOU?'"

This is another adage I never forget as long as I have a memory.

My notes are everywhere for the next several weeks and months. I wrote things down every time a doctor came by, or we visited one as outpatient, but I must have been more distraught than even I realized at the time, because I have found notes on receipts, on the edges of hospital literature, on random pieces of paper, on napkins, and some, yes, in the journals where they all should have been. Some are dated and some are not, so I am reconstructing the next several weeks after Teresa's discharge from that January 3 surgery from a hodgepodge and a haze of memory.

What I know for sure about this next period of time is that we went home and Teresa swelled in her abdomen from the fluid that was diverted there after the surgical and chemical procedures. Already dealing with the fluid in her feet and legs and wearing her compression socks since it was winter, she began to pursue some fashion items to cover her swollen belly, counting on the likelihood that the accumulation of so much ascites (fluid in the abdominal cavity) was temporary. It remained important to her that she look as well as possible. ("So that I can FEEL as well as possible, y'all!") Fashion and cosmetic and esthetic would eventually begin to take a back seat to health and comfort, though, as it was the pursuit of these that was primary and ongoing. Her kidney function began to suffer even further as the fluid filled her tissues and pressed on those abdominal organs. She experienced a myriad of symptoms: off- and on- feelings of nausea, loss of appetite, lack of energy, coughing, high creatinine readings, loss of weight, and STILL the vasospasms with that burning in her chest, incessant burping at times, arms tingling, all... Her blood pressure was trending lower and lower. On January 24 she was readmitted to MUSC and she stayed there until February 16 – twenty-three days!

Chapter 33 Angels of Mercy

During these days of hospitalization in the midst of winter we tried all sorts of things to keep ourselves busy. We were probably on our phones, ipads, and laptops too much. We did walk the halls when Teresa felt that she could. Sometimes we would go out and sit in the sunroom overlooking Charleston and sometimes, when the staff allowed her off the floor, we went downstairs to what we called the solarium. Occasionally someone was playing the piano and there were lots of passersby to observe.

Various members of the heart failure and transplant teams would come by Teresa's room to see her. They remained puzzled but still seemed committed to figuring it out. Because of the ascites in her abdomen, it was necessary to now perform what is known as a paracentesis. This involved guiding, by ultrasound, a tube into the abdominal cavity where the most fluid was accumulating and drawing that out. There was a risk of infection, of puncturing a bowel, of nicking blood vessels, but it was not considered as risky as the thoracenteses (in the lung cavity) as we understood it. So now we were introduced to another area of the hospital at MUSC: radiology. There were wonderful staff there, professional and kind and REAL. They chatted with Teresa about her family and about the work she had done. They shared about their lives and families as well, which made her feel that she was still living in a normal world. Once when Teresa had returned home from the hospital she received a gift in the mail from one of the technicians in radiology. This precious young woman had been to a craft fair/festival and found an item there (as I recall there was a mirror involved with this gift!) and thought to send that to Teresa, who was thrilled.

There were so so many nurses and other staff whose faces will forever be etched in my memory from those dark, agonizing months. As mentioned early in this memoir, I had tried to pray from the beginning for every single person in every job description of the medical world who would ever help Teresa. I would try not to leave anyone out; I'm sure I did but God covered my omissions. I loved to talk to and find out about the lives of those we encountered and we tried to affirm them in the jobs they were doing. While I can never name them all, maybe these can serve as representative of those who "flung the brush of morning against the canvas of the night."

Kara was a nurse who cared that Teresa seemed to be a bit depressed during the long late January/early February hospital stay and arranged to move her to a hospital room with a better view. AND she noticed that Teresa was not eating the hospital food very well, so she stopped at the market and brought in a big fine potato (something Teresa had said she thought she could eat) which she then baked in the staff oven and served to her. There was Sam, who had such a sense of humor and made Teresa laugh. Sam had had triplets and she shared some of that journey with us. Ann also showed a great interest in Teresa, Bradley and Preston and as she had time she and Teresa would share and compare family stories. We never forget Bonnie, who had been with Teresa the night she was transplanted and was finishing her career there on the floor with her beloved cardiac patients: outrageously funny and direct, she made Teresa shake with laughter.

There were wonderful nurse techs at MUSC, many of whom were studying for their RN degrees. I remember one night when Teresa had been inpatient for quite a while and was finally able to walk the halls a bit, one of the young techs called out from the desk, "Mrs. Taylor, we're short-handed tonight. Can you help out?" He was light-heartedly suggesting that she knew the routines almost as well as they did, and that made her smile.

Mrs. Cash was a housekeeper who was also a fine storyteller, philosopher and theologian. She brightened many days. Some of the other housekeepers and transport staff became so familiar with Teresa and our family that they would stop us to give a hug and encouraging word when they encountered us in the halls.

Hwajoo, the beautiful Korean transplant nurse who was often on duty always wanted to make things better for Teresa, as did most of these fine nurses. Hwajoo gave Teresa back rubs, something she had learned from her mother or grandmother as I recall. She was also the one who said one day in clinic that she would give "fashion advice" to Teresa as she began to explore ways to hide the accumulating fluid in her abdomen. She had a lovely quiet reassuring manner and an underlying sense of humor and fun in her demeanor. Katie was the youngest and the newest addition to the nurse transplant coordinator team and she gave birth to a daughter while Teresa was being treated at MUSC during that last year. She would come in and sometimes chat with Teresa (more than just the medical exam and questioning) about her family and experiences and those of Teresa's. Kathy Law was another transplant nurse who showed great concern for Teresa and sincere puzzlement appeared in her sweet face when there did not seem to be answers. I hold in my heart always these faces and those of others who tried so hard.

Chapter 34 More Angels of Mercy

Teresa went home for about eight days but had to be admitted again on February 25 with the ongoing problem with ascites and diminished kidney function. During the months of 2014 I sometimes told Terry when I talked to him from Charleston that I could feel the darkness coming for me. Particularly I felt this when the actual dark was about to blanket the streets outside our window. It was not a sense of evil but rather the sadness and despair of depression I think. We were in a dark place, but Teresa continued to keep her brave face on so I tried to as well. We chatted with everyone who came by. As dismal as the situation seemed, I recall one of the nursing staff coming in to Teresa's room one day and saying, "Ah, man, it's the beach in here!" We wondered how bad it must have been for other patients on the hall. They may have said that in every room, but it made Teresa feel that things could be always worse than they were. I tried to stay thankful and also prayerful for those who were indeed suffering even worse than we were.

I knew there were many family members, friends, acquaintances, and even strangers praying for us. A particular friend comes to mind as I write about the hard times of 2014. Karen Rudd was in my Sunday School class and we had not gotten to know each other well yet, but Karen took me on in a personal, special way. She began sending cards to me by mail, each with an encouraging message. She would show up with a gift bag of surprises at church or send a cake that she had baked. She would text me messages with the most powerful devotional thoughts and record voice messages that began, "Good Morning, Beautiful. I just wanted you to know..." She sent a CD and other items to Teresa. This beautiful spirited friend became to me a kind of lifeline or hotline between me and our Heavenly Father. She was surely Jesus to me in those dark, dark months.

So many found ways to show their caring during that winter and the spring and summer to follow. My childhood friend Sylvia, whose symbolic angel pins and other kind acts had supported me early in the transplant journey, sent a prayer shawl that her church circle had made. Sylvia's daughter and her church friends made a monetary donation to

Teresa's family that helped them with travel and other items needed for the back and forth trips to the hospital. I recall Teresa's friend Barbara from the Lizard's Thicket visiting her at home. Heidi and Holly Storey brought Teresa a Tupperware order, which provided her a chance to catch up with friends from the past and also feel like she was doing an ordinary, normal thing – ordering Tupperware! Another friend Fabi was expecting a baby and Teresa delighted in that and sharing herself with Fabi and planning for Fabi's baby boy between hospital stays. She made one of her astonishing wreaths for Fabi's hospital door when her son was born. Gayle and Sandra, longtime friends from high school and church, made the trip to Charleston several times to visit, chatting about the ordinary and bringing normal into the hospital room with them. The simplest things delighted her and she never forgot a kindness. When she and Bradley would go out to eat, especially at Mellow Mushroom, Teresa often saw her cousin John's daughters, Brooke and Riley, and their mom there. She told me, "Mama, every single time I see those girls they come over and give me a hug. Those are the sweetest girls."

During this visit that began in late February I began to feel that I could never inform every precious one who wanted to know how Teresa was. I had been emailing but would inevitably leave someone off the group list. I would tell her status and then realize I had omitted something. The realization came to me, like it did when I knew I needed to apply for her disability, that I had to do something differently. Teresa had kept up with some very ill friends on Caring Bridge and I had too in the past so we decided together that we would place her story and updates there. She wanted me to write for her, so I wrote her introductory story and then began the journaling. This was a wonderful vehicle for her to post some pictures and comments and read the encouraging words from others. To ALL who ever sent a thought through Caring Bridge I send back to you an affirmation and a thank you – you need to know how very much that meant. She loved getting cards and calls and visits too, of course, but being as confined as she was, that phone that Bradley had gotten her was a lifeline with its fount of texts, messages, emails, and then the Caring Bridge. She was on Facebook for a time too and enjoyed reading and seeing the events in the lives of others that she loved.

While I could write on Caring Bridge about Teresa's progress or setbacks, I tried to choose my words carefully so as not to discourage her, trying to keep alive in her that "something to hope for." I tried not to convey there my mounting despair and my fear that we were losing her. She read every word of every report. As I look through these journals I remain thankful for this platform but my heart breaks for those months of late February through early September. The best I seem to have to offer at this place in our memoir is to glean from those journals and from my painful memories the mighty struggle she made to stay here. We began our Caring Bridge postings on February 26, 2014.

Chapter 35 A Second Transplant?

They stopped Teresa's diuretic around February 26 because her kidney function numbers were not at a good place and until that improved they did not want to resume them. They also wanted to set up the paracentesis procedures somewhere nearer home in Lexington because those would need to be done fairly often to keep the accumulating fluid in her abdomen at a bearable level. The biggest news we got on this late February day was that they wanted to consult her insurance company about the possibility of re-transplant. I recall clearly the day that Dr. Brisco came in with this news. She was a tall beautiful woman always dressed fashionably and wearing high, high heels when she rounded. She was of course a member of the cardiovascular team that treated heart failure and transplant patients, but she had also done significant work related to reno-cardiac (kidney-heart) interactions. While she reminded us that this would be Teresa's second heart transplant, she said that they would also be pursuing a kidney transplant because both organs would be essential for her survival.

When the doctors left after this news, Teresa and I both cried. When I asked her how she felt, Teresa said, "I'm scared, yes, but I want it. I want to feel like I felt for those ten+ years."

My reply was, "Me, too!"

When I went out a few minutes later to ask the nurse for something, Teresa said, "Now, Mama, DON'T go out there crying!"

My Caring Bridge entry for February 26 ended, "That's our brave girl. We and our all-sufficient God are planning to go the distance. PLEASE and THANK YOU for praying." There was an outpouring of support in Caring Bridge comments when we began to journal.

They wasted no time beginning Teresa's evaluation for her transplants. Insurance approved the process immediately. February 27 was a busy day. A number of tests were involved in transplantation evaluation, some of which we remembered from the first transplant and some that we didn't. Teresa went first to the pulmonary lab for the lung tests, which involved drawing blood from an artery and a set of breathing tests - inhaling, exhaling, holding breath, trying to empty lungs, etc. We had been back just a while when they took her for a CT scan of her head. We returned to the room for a while longer and then they came for her to go for a vessel test (carotid, etc. in neck), then straight from there we went to the ultrasound department for an ultrasound of the vessels in her abdomen - kidney, liver, etc. She had a lot of wheelchair rides on this day.

When we returned to the room after this last test we found a team of lung doctors waiting to look at her lungs with an ultrasound machine. The doctor was very nice and, of course, very smart. He said their job was to let the transplant team know of the risks involved from a lung perspective He said the levels of risk were mild, moderate, and high - for pneumonia, infection, etc. Teresa was young, had not smoked, had no severe allergies, no COPD, no asbestos exposure. She had had those two right lung cavity procedures performed in early January, however, and she did have a mild pleural effusion in her left lung cavity still. He believed her risk would be moderate and they would recommend some things for post-surgery to try to minimize the risks as much as possible.

We thought we were through. Teresa ordered a couple of things from food service that she thought she could eat. This was when I usually went downstairs to get a bowl of soup or something. I did that and when I got back two of the ladies from the lab were in her room to get 15 (or portions thereof) vials of blood from her. I felt sure this was for donor matching, blood and tissue typing, antibody levels, etc. They were praising her bravery and even saying she had found the best vessel in her arm for them to use.

All of this information and the tests yet to be performed would have to go before the transplant team for their consideration. It would be a group decision to seek the transplant(s) for her or not. They would have to come to an agreement based on all test results. We surely did pray that Teresa would get this chance if it was what God wanted.

We missed the nephrologist who had come by earlier in the day. Teresa's kidney function had continued to decline and the cardiologist who had rounded that morning said they were asking nephrology to come by. Since we took so many field trips, they missed us, but we expected to see them the next day. Dr. Brisco had said when she was here during the day that they may have to do dialysis (along with the paracentesis procedures for the fluid buildup) until transplant if the kidneys continued to decline, but the nephrologist was to give us more information.

The next day, February 28, Teresa had a treadmill stress test, saw a nutritionist as well as one of the kidney transplant doctors, a social worker, and, of course, the cardiologists. She did not have much energy at all and was nauseated in the late afternoon. Dr. Brisco was really anxious for the regular nephrologists to see her because she wanted to know if dialysis was warranted and if it could be done. It was hard for Teresa to eat with all of the fluid she was holding on to. Sometimes if she got the food down she could not hold onto it. The surgeons wanted her to be as nourished as possible if they decided they could transplant her. The nephrologists did get by later in the day and decided they wanted, with Cardiology's approval, to resume some of the diuretics and try to improve the kidney function that way before doing something more drastic. I realize now that they did not see her as a good candidate for dialysis, which lowers blood pressure even further and generally takes a toll on the body. We asked for prayers on Caring Bridge for the whole process and for Teresa's kidneys and nutrition. This was way bigger than us!

On March 1 Teresa was still eating very little and her creatinine number had come down by only one tenth of a point; cardiologists and nephrologists did agree on adding some diuretics back to her meds regimen. I could tell she was feeling a bit low. Her cheerful Edwards cousins, J.K. and Ann's families, visited and some other Lexington friends, Shaunta and Jess, as well, and she surely loved seeing everyone - that helped to get us through that day. We took some pictures, which she always cherished and usually posted on Caring Bridge. I regret those times that we did not take pictures (forgetting, iPad not charged, etc.), but I remind myself that it is good to be in the moment and not behind the camera so very much too.

Some of the Taylor family visited the next afternoon and we enjoyed that – we sat in the waiting room as we had done the day before with our visitors. Our Preston was among these special visitors. We were thankful, as mentioned earlier, for the many staff who were taking care of Teresa. There was one housekeeper that we had met during a prior visit on another floor who was one of the hardest working, most happy-faced people you could hope to meet. We would greet each other in the hallways and in Teresa's room. She was on Teresa's floor with a group of folks this afternoon of March 2 and when we saw each other we fell into a hug in the hallway. She had not seen Teresa in her room, asked about her, and chased her down in the waiting room to give her a hug. I thank God for Cassandra even today and again, for all of those she represents - getting their assigned jobs done so cheerfully and making a difference for those who need it.

Although I cannot call all the names, I want to insert a giant thanks right here to **everyone** who ever came to visit Teresa at MUSC, both family and friends. Whether aunts, uncles, cousins (Edwards, Power, Taylor), church friends, other friends, community acquaintances, work associates, or other connection, please know how much it meant to our girl. Teresa's cousin Robert would slip in occasionally with his quiet strength, often bringing something his wife Chris wanted to send. Sometimes Chris and Robert's sister Margaret came too. John and Missy gave to Teresa and Bradley a gift certificate to eat out at some choice Charleston restaurants, again injecting hope for a future when she would have her appetite back. Dwayne, one of our ministers, would bring his lively self there almost any time he was in the area and brighten things up. Other church friends, Bradley's chaplain from Southeastern, and Ricky, who was another Southeastern Christian friend, seemed to show up at just the right moment. Charleston is not an easy city in which to drive and MUSC parking, while efficient, was not always easy to navigate, particularly at certain times. I value everyone who made it there in person, as well as all of you who ever breathed a prayer, texted, emailed, called, sent cards, commented on Caring Bridge or Facebook. I know that was God breathing life into Teresa through all of these gestures of encouragement. I weep with gratitude even now as I think on these acts of compassion.

Chapter 36 Bestowing the Title "Warrior Princess"

A few days after the blood draw that was done for transplant evaluation, I came in to Teresa's hospital room to find her arms covered in bruises. With so many varying medicines to take and so many conditions to fight, along with both intravenous and injectable and blood-extracting needles, it was bound to show up on her thin little arms. She had not complained but it broke my heart and when I saw the expanse of bruises, I said to her, "Teresa, you are our warrior princess." We were waiting on her like a princess at times by now, but she was still fighting with all she had to get back to better health. When I bestowed her new nickname on her, she smiled rather wanly and said, "I like that."

By the morning of March 2 Teresa's creatinine had come down some and they gave her Lasix in an IV to see if they could move it even more in a positive direction. Terry and I went out that afternoon to find a robe for Teresa and also to give her and Bradley some time together. Of course that is when the docs came in with their plan for the immediate future. They planned to give her the protein which she continued to need because of her lack of appetite and consequently poor nutrition. They would do another paracentesis while she was in the hospital, watch her kidney function a bit longer, make a plan for outpatient paracentesis, and eventually get her home for a while.

I wrote this in our Caring Bridge journal on March 2:

"We think most of the testing for the transplant workup has been completed. The results may be presented to the team as early as this week. Please pray that Teresa will be accepted if this is the miracle God is planning. We do not rule out other miracles, but it seems the doctors are thinking this is the best option if the test results are favorable. Continue to know, family and friends, that your prayers make a difference for us. Like Paul said, 'I thank my God upon every remembrance of you.' Philippians 1:3 (KJV) And if you are among those we have not met but you are loving us with your prayers, we feel you with us here too, and we count you among our blessings."

By the next morning Teresa's creatinine was down another ½ point and the doctors were happy. It was still not down to her baseline but they hoped it would decrease further and they gave her more diuretics by IV. They planned to drain fluid the following day and infuse some protein and see by the day after that how her kidneys would react. The nursing staff were searching for a facility in Lexington that could perform the paracentesis procedures and infusions, probably on a weekly basis. We were hoping all of the above could happen so we could get Teresa home where she so, so wanted to be. We asked Caring Bridge readers for prayers for her to be able to eat more and gain some strength and energy so she could continue to fight the fight.

On March 4 they drained 3.1 liters of fluid off in the paracentesis. Teresa and I walked around and around the halls during the afternoon and she felt that she could eat more for dinner that night. We were very thankful for that and also for the news that her kidney labs were slightly better. They did give her the protein infusion after the drain but no diuretics. We were hoping, based on these steps forward, that they could send her home with short- and long- term plans and that is exactly what happened the next day, March 5. She would return to clinic on March 12 for them to check her progress.

I then recorded this in our Caring Bridge journal on March 4:

"Some have asked how to pray specifically. Besides the prayer for overall healing, by whatever miracle God chooses, please pray that the fluid does not return so quickly and that her kidneys can stay stable. Also, we met a man at the end of the hall who had gotten 20 pints of blood. He received a liver transplant in 1997 but there is a problem with bone marrow now, I believe he said. He was waiting to be discharged while we chatted with him. He said, 'You have to keep believing. You CAN'T stop!'

Chapter 37 More Hospital, More Wait

On March 9 Teresa had been home for four days and she had been eating a bit more and although still fatigued she did seem to have more energy than she had had a week earlier. She even drove the car a short distance one day and while Bradley was at home over the weekend, they had Preston's friend Ryan over to spend the night. This was a great treat for Preston. On Sunday night Pop and I kept Preston at our house and that was a treat for us! We had been doing this on a fairly regular basis and with the prolonged hospital stays we had missed out on those adventures with him.

While we did not yet have the results from the first evaluative tests for the second transplant, we assumed the transplant team would soon have those results and would begin their preliminary discussions about her acceptance before so long. We thought that perhaps we might hear some news at that next clinic visit which was scheduled for the following Wednesday. At church on that Sunday morning so many people said to Terry and me, "We have surely been praying for Teresa," to which we expressed our gratitude and asked them to – yet again – please not stop doing just that.

Teresa did not make it uneventfully to the following Wednesday which was when her outpatient visit was scheduled. During the night of Sunday, March 9, she had vasospasms off and on all during the night. We headed back to MUSC on Monday morning and they saw her in the chest pain center (a kind of emergency room for heart patients). They said they would be admitting her but that the hospital was full at the time. About 5:30 that afternoon a room became available and she went to the fifth floor. They had run tests in the ER, including blood work, and we did learn from some of those labs that her creatinine was down – good news for kidney function –and the night nurse looked up her troponin level (an indicator of heart muscle damage) and did not find it elevated. This made us guardedly optimistic that she had not suffered a heart attack, but they would draw it two more times during the following hours to see if it spiked. The last time she had had a similar episode the troponin **had** gone up, indicating some injury to the heart muscle. The cardiologists had not rounded before Terry and I left the hospital so we did not know what the other findings were. Bradley wanted to stay the night with Teresa in case she had a reoccurrence of the vasospasms. We slept at my brother's James Island house, returning to MUSC the following morning.

That morning did not start well for Teresa, as she had several runs of what the doctors were assuming were those vasospasms again. She did feel some better as the day passed. Dr. Craig reported that he did not see further sustained heart damage at this point, at least from what he called the "objective data," which we assumed meant things like the troponin level not being elevated and the EKG not being aberrant, at least for her. They sent the pacemaker interrogator in and he checked her pacemaker, which seemed to be doing what it was programmed to do. We were thankful for that.

Dr. Craig said he did not want to do another heart cath because of how that procedure seemed to impact her kidneys, which were doing somewhat better by this point. So his plan was to observe her for a time as inpatient, have the ultrasound staff see if they needed to drain fluid the next day as originally scheduled, then make a plan to get her home again. He also said he wanted to expedite the testing for the second transplant, but the main three remaining tests were to be outpatient and at least two of them would be done in Lexington most likely when she was well enough to schedule them. Then when all results were in, her case could be presented to the team.

They drew 2.5 liters of fluid from Teresa, which was somewhat less than the prior week, and then they gave her protein by infusion again. Dr. Craig upped the vasospasm medicine slightly and took her off of another medicine that she had been taking just since the last hospital stay, since he said it could cause her to hold onto fluid. He asked her if she wanted to go home. She said, "I am ready to go home right now." That did not happen instantly, but in a few hours they did get her discharge papers ready and we got back to Lexington about 6:45 that evening. We were thankful on this day that her kidney function was still good and that she did not seem to have any significant vasospasms. We asked our Caring Bridge followers to please pray that the vasospasms would stay away and that Teresa would hold onto less and less of the ascites. We also needed prayer for the expedition of the transplant evaluation process, that she would be accepted as a candidate for re-transplantation, and that those things that needed to happen before, during and after that process could be accomplished as smoothly as possible. We also prayed for the strength we read about in Isaiah 40:31.

Teresa had six days at home, puttering around her house, straightening up, shopping briefly on a few occasions, and orchestrating the painting (Bradley), pickup /cleanup (Preston and me) and planning of Preston's soon-to-be rearranged and redecorated bedroom. She was moving him from the little boy theme to the big boy theme in there and he and she were excited despite her low energy level and lack of appetite as well as some fairly aggravating coughing spells.

She and I returned to Charleston on March 18 in order to make her clinic appointment the next day and for her to have yet another paracentesis. We ran out in the evening to pick up something to eat and take it back to the house. While we were out we were passed by that car about which we sometimes say, "I hope they make it" because of speed or other driving factors. Usually all turns out okay but this time it did not. We saw the car and some of its injured occupants in the front yard of a home a short distance ahead where it had careened off the road. A reminder to both of us of how quickly life can change. We asked our Caring Bridge friends to pray for those involved as well as for Teresa's appointment the next day.

Teresa saw Dr. Crumbley in clinic on the 19th. She always loved Dr. C. He was, of course, the one who had transplanted her and while he no longer operated he was often the one in clinic during this time. He was always kind, caring, and so very funny, which always pleased Teresa. His advice on this day was, "The Twiggy look is getting old! You HAVE to start eating more!" So they adjusted her diet to about anything within reason that she wanted to eat and could keep down. "Snack all day like the gorillas do!" he told her. Her kidney number was still down which was good news and the fluid draw they did was only 1.5 liters, which was less than the week before and also good news. We did not hear from the chest x-ray results or from the labs they had drawn before we left, but we were just glad she was good enough TO leave. She was still coughing a good bit still but they did not hold us there for that

When they called Teresa on March 21 they told her they were increasing one of her immunosuppressant drugs and that Dr. Crumbley wanted a CT scan of her left lung because of the look of the effusion on the chest x-ray. It would be a hospital admission because of the vulnerability of her kidneys. They had also gotten the paperwork and other approvals done for her to begin having the paracentesis procedures done weekly at Lexington Medical Center nearby to us. She expected to start there the following week but other events transpired before that could happen.

On March 23 we begged our Caring Bridge friends for prayer once again as we headed toward MUSC because of chest pain off and during yet another night. Bradley drove Teresa ahead and Terry and I followed in our car. They admitted her to ICU this time. They said they would most likely be administering drugs that were more easily given in that unit. Her chest pain subsided some once we got there. They set about the testing process, drawing labs, doing a 12-lead EKG, checking blood pressure and oxygen levels, etc. They found her troponin elevated somewhat and because of that they began to treat her for a mild heart attack. They attached a heparin drip in one arm and prepared the other side for a nitro drip if it became necessary. I decided to stay and sent Bradley and Terry off to sleep. Bradley was nearly sleepwalking – I think neither he nor Teresa had slept much at all the night before. She did feel like eating a portion of a salad for dinner and was able to sit up in bed to do that. We kept reminding ourselves that "God has a plan."

They moved her to a regular room from ICU the following afternoon, March 24. The troponin did not continue to rise so we assumed the damage to the heart muscle was not extreme. Except for some fleeting heartburn in the morning she felt better during the day. She did not move around so much but she was able to eat. They kept the heparin drip on her and told us that since she was already inpatient with this recent episode they wanted the CT scan of that lung. It was scheduled for the next day.

On March 25 they gave Teresa IV fluids ahead of her having the CT scan so that maybe her kidneys would not be injured by the contrast she had to have for that. Then that night after the scan they gave her extra diuretic in hopes of helping her eliminate the dye from her system. If they put too much fluid on her it could cause shortness of breath and other symptoms, and if not enough, her kidneys would not function properly to throw off the dye. There was a delicate balance between heart and kidney function, which we had learned but would come to realize even more painfully in the months ahead. The goal during this particular hospital stay was for the kidneys to function well and recover quickly from receiving the contrast.

The next day she got still more diuretics. She **had** retained too much of the fluid and her kidney numbers began to reflect it. She was able to eat some, though, and kept it down, for which we were thankful. They spoke of doing another paracentesis in a few days if necessary.

They interrogated her pacemaker in the afternoon. We did not know they were planning to do this, so something on her monitor may have concerned them. The one who ran the test said the pacemaker seemed to be working okay.

On March 28 they did do a paracentesis, draining 3.2 liters of fluid out of her. Her kidney markers had risen further and they wanted to get those down. We also found out that day that the CT scan they had done to see how the pleural effusion looked had revealed an enlarged lymph node. This was a new worry. I could not say the word on Caring Bridge because of alarming Teresa, but I knew they would be looking for cancer and they scheduled a PET scan for the following Monday morning to explore it further.

Chapter 38 Good News/Bad News

By March 30 Teresa's creatinine had gone up again and they called in the kidney doctors. They began doing several things to attempt to get it down and avoid dialysis. She did not feel like eating much and seemed to keep a feeling of nausea and malaise. The following morning there was another slight bump upward in the lab work but the cardiologists and the kidney doctors both said that since it was such a slight increase, it might be plateauing and could begin to come down some. Sure enough, by five o'clock it was down by half a point. While it had a long way to go to be back to her recent baseline, we were thankful that the downward trend had started. They added a couple of meds for kidney function to her regimen and some diuretics.

On March 31 she had the PET scan. We did not hear results immediately. They came to her room and did a kidney ultrasound during that day also. She was able to walk three times around the hall in the late afternoon, which was major compared to how she had been feeling.

On April 1 we learned that the PET scan had shown no lymphoma in Teresa's abdomen and the scan of her kidney had shown no obstruction of blood flow to the kidneys. The PET scan, which had been from the top of her head to below her knees, **did** show some enlargement of her thyroid gland and they now wanted to schedule a sonogram of that in the near future, but the endocrinologist thought it could most likely be managed with follow-up to check for any changes.

Her renal function seemed to be be slowly improving, but she was still holding onto fluid, getting lots of diuretics as well as supplements for some minerals and other nutrients that were depleted. Everyone wanted her to eat more, as she had lost far too much weight by now, but her appetite was just not there. We were managing to get a few hundred calories in her each day.

We rejoiced on this day in the good news of no cancer showing in the scan. Indeed we did not want that complication; however, the source of the ascites remained a mystery.

Over the next several days we just hung out waiting for that creatinine number to get to a place that Teresa could manage at home.

Oh, how she wanted to go home! We had a scare with her potassium level one day. It showed up so very low in the morning lab work that her sweet nurses were almost frantic to get some potassium into her by IV. We were wary of anything more going in by IV because of the added fluid, but they said they needed to get the number up as quickly as possible. They said it might burn some when it ran through the IV line going in, and sure enough, when they started the first bag, she could not stand it. "It feels like my whole arm is broken," she said. So they did stop the IV potassium and gave her some big old pills which did get the number up some. We were glad she did not have to have those six little bags of fluid over six hours through the IV. They scanned her thyroid gland that same afternoon and we expected to hear from that before we left the hospital.

They had to do another paracentesis on April 3, drawing 3.4 liters of fluid off. She was always able to eat a bit more after the procedure and that made everyone happy. By April 6 they had transitioned her from IV diuretics to oral and told her they could let her go! They did want to do a needle biopsy of her thyroid gland but said they could schedule her for an outpatient appointment to do that. So we were Lexington-bound at last, with a change in diuretic and a change in beta blocker and the addition of another couple of drugs. She was looking so forward to sleeping in her own bed.

While she was back in Lexington Teresa had labs drawn locally and I was able to run her around for a few other brief errands. She took on fluid again and could not eat much. She had her first paracentesis procedure at Lexington Medical Center. She was apprehensive because all of the others had been done in Charleston, but everyone there at LMC was very kind, efficient, and professional. They drew 5 ¾ liters from her, the most yet in any paracentesis. We suspected some of the ascites might be from right-sided heart failure, but we were hoping that the fluid from the duct ligation would eventually "find its pathway" as we had been told and she would experience relief. We could feel the prayers of the angels and warriors and that kept us going.

We had also asked for prayer on Caring Bridge about this time for my brother Raiford who was undergoing treatment for metastasized cancer. My heart was heavy over this as he lived a distance away and we could not often visit, but we knew prayer could sustain him, move him forward, and that God had a plan for him too. His situation looked grim to us, but we don't see through God's eyes, do we? I have thought often of the tapestry that God's plan has been referred to, that overall work of art which is woven from the threads of His creations. We DO see through a glass darkly now, but later, oh my... I am counting on it.

On April 15 Teresa had another MUSC appointment. Her creatinine was elevated once again, which disappointed her, but the doc said that it was probably fluctuating - up and down - along with the fluid accumulation and drain procedures. He tweaked a couple of her medicines. He also wanted her to eat more, to "onload calories," even if she had to eat foods containing fat to do so. (She had been off of all fats for a while when they were treating the chylous effusion.) As the fluid built, she would have less and less appetite. She was scheduled for the drain at Lexington Medical Center for the following Friday again.

The great sadness reported in this day of my Caring Bridge journal was some news we had received not long before this appointment. We had been trying to process this before reporting it: "They have told Teresa her case is of too high risk a nature for the present transplant program at MUSC." We had wondered about this because we kept thinking we should have heard the committee's findings sooner. The lab work showed that Teresa's antibodies were at 99% - way too high for consideration at MUSC. There was a procedure that could bring them down some – but it was not often attempted in a second transplant from what we were understanding. One of the doctors had discussed with her the possibility of asking Emory in Atlanta to consider her case. We knew she needed to get a few more things in order (thyroid biopsy, some weight gain, and a couple of other possible appointments) for Emory to agree to see her, or maybe even before they would be asked to see her.

Preston had gone with us to MUSC for this appointment. (He was out of school for spring break.) He was in on everything she had done that day. We think he heard that his mom's kidney function had slipped some again. We think he heard their surprise at the amount of fluid she had had drawn off the previous Friday. He heard Dr. Crumbley say that she needed to gain calories/weight and some of the ways to accomplish that (even Krispy Kreme, his favorite!). When they got back home, his Nana, Bradley's mother, came by their house to see them. He took her to his room to show her what his daddy had done in there while he was gone (painting, etc.) and while she was in there with him, he told her,

"Nana, we got good news today! Mama can eat ANYthing she wants!" He chose to focus on that **good** news – a lesson to me for sure.

I wrote this in my Caring Bridge journal on April 17: "Dear friends, what a reminder (Preston's remarks to Nana) of all those things we need to be thankful for! Sometimes when I get on my knees, I try not to ask God for anything, just thank Him for ALL that He has done. Last night was one of those nights. This morning I am still thanking (and back to begging too!)." We reminded ourselves yet again that GOD HAS A PLAN!

Chapter 39 Ongoing Ascites Mystery

Teresa was by now going for the paracentesis procedures at Lexington Medical Center once a week. They were not as painful as time passed, or at least she was getting more used to them. They were averaging about 3.5 liters of fluid draw each week. We were getting to know the staff there and they were wonderful. I think back now and newly appreciate that they chatted with her about ordinary things even as they must have pondered the fate of this young mother who was undergoing this procedure so often. They talked to her about her child and theirs, things happening in the world, on TV, etc. I recall one of the techs during the procedure admiring Teresa's ring - it was a big flashy thing – and Teresa looked down at it admiringly herself and then looked up and replied, "Well, thank you. It's fake!" That brought a laugh and laughter was definitely something she (and they) could use!

Between mid-April and early May Teresa seemed to rally a bit even amongst lab work and paracentesis procedures. She drove her car occasionally, picking up Preston from school a day or so, taking me along as a passenger. We thought the fact that Dr. Crumbley had told her she could eat the unrestricted diet might have something to do with all of this. When she returned to MUSC in early May for appointments that were scheduled with three different doctors (cardiologist, pulmonologist, and gastroenterologist) as well as a paracentesis to be done there, her labs showed that her creatinine was down and that she was beginning to build some protein back into her system, as a result, we think, of somewhat better nutrition. Both of these were good indicators. The amount of fluid taken out was slightly less than it had been prior, also good.

The bad news though, was that the fluid they drew in this paracentesis was turning milky again, a result of the increased fat they had allowed her to eat. The fluid was a different color when she ate the reduced-fat diet. So we had the "Catch-22." While the docs were glad the fluid catch was less, they were very concerned about the nutrients she was losing with the procedure each week. They had been struggling for a long time now with just what could be causing all of the ascites.

They and we continually hoped for the fluid to find those "new lymphatic venous connections" and we all knew that could take months to happen. However, things were getting so urgent with weight and nutritional issues that they now wanted her to see a hepatologist (liver doctor) and have the pressures checked in her liver. There is a kind of cirrhosis that is known as "cardiac-induced cirrhosis" which can occur if high pressures in the heart transfer high pressure to the liver, causing hardening and also causing the lymphatic vessels to break down. I think they wanted to see if the liver was the source of the ascites she kept accumulating. They told her they would schedule her appointment and call her regarding the date and time. We returned to Lexington.

Chapter 40 A Happy Keeper Memory Amidst Continued Struggle

In May there were several occasions that Teresa looked forward to. Bradley's birthday and Melinda's were in May, and Teresa and Bradley's anniversary was too. A new event joined the month of May when Bradley's brother's little daughter Sederis was born in 2013. Even though so very sick Teresa wanted to participate in all of these celebrations. One of the last times I can remember we nearly lost our breath from laughing involved shopping for one of these May occasions. I believe it was late in April that we embarked on this task.

Sederis was to have her first birthday party in May of 2014 and Teresa **had** to have the perfect gift for her. She had in her mind this little swimming pool that had some water splasher to it – I cannot recall all of the details except that Teresa had her mind and heart set on this present. We were pushing her in a wheelchair – a small one that was called a transport chair - to shop by this time. As I remember we had already unsuccessfully tried a store or two when we found the swimming pool in a local Walmart. I was carrying my purse, Teresa's purse, and I was pushing. This swimming pool was not in a little box when we located it on the shelf. It was flat, but several feet across both length and width, a big old square really.

I said, "Umm, Ree, I may need to come back later to retrieve this for you. It might be more than we can manage right now. It's a bit bigger than I thought."

"NO, Mama, I have to get it now. It might be gone later. Come on, now. We can do this."

"Right. Sure. And how?"

"I want you to lay that box across the arms of this chair and I am going to hold it on here until we get to the register."

"Teresa, that is NOT going to work. I will get it later today. I promise."

"Heave it on here, Mama."

So I did. I still had the purses and I began to guide the chair with Teresa and the swimming pool in and on it. She was latched on to the box with her fingers barely clawed onto the outer edges. I began to gain some hope a few yards up through the aisles that we could get it done. I did chide her by saying, "Teresa, people are going to see us doing this and say, 'Look at that woman making her disabled daughter carry that package for her. Some people...'" This struck Teresa as one of the funniest things she had heard lately. She began to laugh and when Teresa laughed, she shook and sometimes cried these big old laughter tears too. I guess it was what we have heard described as a belly laugh, not so much loud but deep and nearly uncontrollable. She would get control of herself for a moment and then think on the object of her laughter again and start all over. When she did this it affected and infected the laugh button of whoever she was with. Both of us were laughing so hard when we finally got through paying for this swimming pool and starting out of the store that people probably REALLY were wondering about us by then. How I did it I don't know, but I managed to mine my purse or hers, both of which were still hanging off of me, for a cellphone and took a picture of Teresa clutched onto this box as we were leaving the store. I knew this was a keeper memory.

The weeks of early May rocked along with the usual paracenteses at Lexington Medical Center, each one averaging over three liters. Teresa did not often feel well and strong but she was able to eat out for Bradley's birthday, run a few errands as I chauffeured, and together we took Preston for a pediatrician's appointment. We did not hear when the hepatologist in Charleston would see her, but we did have an appointment on May 22 for the endocrinologist at MUSC to look at that enlarged thyroid gland they had found in the scan.

The endocrinologist, when we had that appointment, did not feel the thyroid was an emergency but did want to biopsy it. They scheduled that for the summer. Teresa got her paracentesis in Charleston on May 22 also since she was there for that appointment anyway. On May 23, 2014 I reported to our Caring Bridge readers:

"Some of you may have seen on the news that MUSC has voluntarily halted all adult heart transplants there temporarily in order to explore why the recent transplants have not been as successful as in the past. One of Teresa's doctors had told us of this problem when he said they would not transplant her there. We still do not yet know if they have approached Emory about her case. Thanks for continuing to pray, for not giving up."

We were reminded at that May appointment of the annual heart cath that was scheduled for June 24. They told her they would be sending some medicine in late May or early June that she was to take ahead of that cath to help protect her kidneys. After the weekly paracentesis (usually at Lexington Medical Center unless she was at MUSC for another appointment anyway) and the albumin infusion she was getting to boost that protein, Teresa almost always felt better in the days immediately after. They had some difficulty late in May with getting the fluid to drain sufficiently. It would drain only so much and then stop. On May 30 they did their best and got 1.9 liters, which seemed encouraging by the numbers but Teresa was still swollen afterward with fluid. The following week they got over three liters and she felt better overall for several days after, as the pattern had become.

Chapter 41 Vanna: This Bond That We Share

I was riding out to Teresa and Bradley's house 'most days while Bradley worked to do what I could to help, whether doing laundry, cleaning, playing with Preston, coaxing her to eat something, taking Preston and/or her somewhere if she felt like it, etc. When Preston was out of school he sometimes went to a local summer day camp a few days a week so he could play with other kids, do some athletic things and otherwise have some summer fun.

On the morning of June 4 I got up and prepared Terry's breakfast and he got the newspaper from the box as was our routine. He brought it in and we ate and began to read. I finished the front section of the paper and picked up the Palmetto section, perusing the obituaries. My world reeled as I saw that Vanna Dorn, the darling who was transplanted just two weeks before Teresa, had lost her fight.

We had encountered Vanna and her mother at MUSC a few years before and we knew that Vanna was having some problems. She and Teresa had reconnected on Facebook and swapped some of their concerns. Vanna had been told at MUSC some time before Teresa that she was not eligible for retransplant either. Teresa took on that sorrow as her own, even before she received the same denial for herself. They were a great support for each other.

My last happy memory with Vanna sprung to my mind immediately, along with the tears that also began to flow for her and her family. Vanna and Teresa had chatted when they were at clinic at MUSC not so many months earlier. We had casually mentioned parking sometimes being an issue and Vanna insisted that we pursue a handicap placard for our car that would ease this burden. She told us how to go about that and we fully intended to pursue it. Before we could, though, Vanna and her mom solved our problem. The next time Teresa was admitted at MUSC Vanna somehow found out and into the room she rolled in her wheelchair with her mom pushing, exuberantly holding up the parking application for us to fill out and have signed by staff. She made the whole process so much easier for us and I never parked my car there again that I did not think of her and that gift. I had never seen

Vanna when she was not full of cheer and chatter – I know she must have had some hard, hard times, but she only ever showed sunshine to me.

I knew I had to get to Teresa and tell her this news about Vanna and I did not even know how to begin. I did not do very well. I remember getting there and Teresa was sitting in the den in her recliner. I made some small talk before sitting down right on the floor in front of her chair. I said something like, "Ree, Vanna didn't make it. I saw in today's newspaper that she's left us." She looked at me incredulously for only a second or two before her heart completely broke and she began to sob. She soon wanted to know why and how and exactly when and where and I did not know 'most of those answers. Vanna's younger brother wrote a beautiful tribute to her on Facebook and Teresa eventually was able to read that. She also composed a lovely verse/ tribute of her own to Vanna, complete with a "heart" she designed, posting it to Facebook or Caring Bridge as a "tribute to an amazing young lady and my friend. Vanna and I were transplanted 10 days apart. I miss you so much, baby girl. You remain in my heart. I will never forget the bright light and inspiration you always will be.

Heart 2 Heart journey
Right from the start...
Moments together,
Moments apart...
Proudly we have
Scars that we wear...
Nothing can break
This bond that we share."

Vanna was buried on Friday, June 6. Teresa was scheduled for yet another drain at Lexington Medical Center at the time of the funeral. She wanted to go by the funeral home before the appointment so we did and I pushed her in. No one had arrived yet for us to speak to, so we signed the guest book and watched the video that was playing in the chapel. There on the screen, among other priceless memories, was the picture of Vanna and Teresa in physical therapy those many years ago, nine and twenty-four years old, PT pals, beginning their journey toward better health.

After the paracentesis procedure Teresa said, "Mama, take me by the cemetery," so I did. They were closing Vanna's grave, and while we had missed the funeral services, Teresa somehow felt that she had gotten as close as she could get that day to Vanna and all she loved considering the circumstances. She continued to reach for understanding about how Vanna could be gone, wanting to go back in time I think to "will" her to stay if that makes sense. A big, big loss for Teresa.

Chapter 42 The Normal, Still, Amidst Growing Problems

I think back on the ordinary things Teresa and I were able to do that late spring and early summer and I will always be thankful for the simplest of tasks that we accomplished together. She wanted me to help her totally clean out her closet. She had clothes in there of every imaginable size it seemed. She sat on her bed and I would bring things out and hold them up. We had our three piles of "Donate it," "Throw it Away," and "Keep it." She had lost so much weight that the "donate" pile and "throw it" pile were accumulating the most by far. She had some clothes there from a trip we had taken her on to the Black and White Market. A couple of things still had the tags on them. She said, "I WANT to wear that, but..." She now had the problem of things fairly recently bought being too large for her, an opposite problem from the past. We laughed uneasily over some of those clothes but tried to believe that this was an ordinary closet purging and we were saving some things for better times. She had been buying smaller and smaller jeans and pants with blousy tops for the swelling in her abdomen.

Another day she wanted to organize her craft supplies. She had bought these perfect containers – a big handled case with trays and some other big containers with drawers to hold her ribbons, wires, glue guns, sequins, etc. She had taken up wreath-making and bow- and barrette-making when she could no longer move around so much. Always an organizer, she could make sense and order of 'most any chaos when she felt good and had a goal. We sat at her kitchen bar and sorted through those things until she had it all arranged at the tips of her fingers so that when she felt able she still could create her beautiful crafts. She also labeled Preston's shelves in his closet so that he knew where things were to go. Just little signs like "short-sleeved knit shirts" and "shorts" and "hoodies" for his wire cubbies made such a difference when putting up his laundry.

Preston had gotten adept at wheeling his mom around in her little transport chair. One day in early June stands out in my memory. It was just a simple little excursion, but these were the best ones it seemed. Teresa wanted to get out of the house for a bit and there was a Dollar General Store not far from their house. I don't recall that there was a specific item that she wanted to buy. Preston and I got the chair and all of us in the car, and even though Preston was not really fond of shopping he wanted to make his mom happy so he was all cooperative and suave. When we got into the store he was totally in control of his mama and that little wheelchair. He slipped into his nine-year old comedian persona, joking with her as he turned each aisle, making her laugh like she had on that swimming pool trip. Sometimes he would sway the wheelchair just a little bit or drive her close to a rack of clothes on purpose to tease her. I hope he can always remember the happiness he brought to her, and this silly outing was just one tiny example of that happiness.

Teresa **wanted** to walk and felt that if she could it would help her general condition overall. Her problem with walking was not totally a strength or even an endurance problem, though those both certainly were issues. Her greatest hindrance was that the fluid retention that she had experienced in her abdomen since the thoracic duct ligation in January had exerted pressure on all of those lower organs. It felt as it everything in her gut was pushing out some days and she had experienced an awful rectal prolapse which was causing her major problems, among them the loss of her mobility. She felt that she could walk hardly any distance.

She had been referred to Dr. Kerry Hammond, a colon and rectal surgeon at MUSC. Dr. Hammond was young (well, certainly to me, she was), caring, careful, and thorough, and I would surely place her on a list of the best of the doctors we saw at MUSC throughout the years. You could see her thinking when she got all of the facts she needed lined up. I never saw anyone seem like she wanted to help a patient any more than she seemed to want to help Teresa. She had seen Teresa in her office early on in this diagnosis of the prolapse and she saw her in the hospital again during this upcoming difficult summer. You could see "the wheels turning" as the saying goes when she did an exam and read the data. She did not draw out (make us wait for) her conclusions, yet we never felt it was a snap decision but rather a carefully thoughtful one. I remember her saying what amounted to, "I want to help you, but you are a high risk surgery right now, Teresa. And aside from the risks, I think if we attempted a surgical fix, the problem would reoccur. I will consider a minimal procedure, though, but let's see how your overall health improves toward that goal." So we marched into that future too with the hope Dr. Hammond offered, albeit small. We did not feel she had let us down really, because she made us feel that she was still in the race with us. It was a race toward losing this dreadful ascites, gaining some weight and improving nutrition. Teresa was starving, I felt, though no one had used that word.

Chapter 43 Liver Troubles Explored

Teresa was scheduled for the right heart cath at MUSC on Tuesday morning, June 24. She was scheduled for both left and right cath, but she called in advance to question the left cath particularly since it involved that dreaded dye, which impacted her kidneys. They called back to say, in light of her concerns, it was to be right side only. They wanted to check the pressures in her heart.

They had drawn less fluid from her in the couple of paracenteses leading up to this cath, although after one of those she had, as earlier, felt that she still retained more fluid than she liked. We saw a little increase in her appetite, though, and were hopeful for some weight gain eventually.

She made it through the heart cath just fine. The doctor said the pressures in her heart were not significantly different from the pressures in the December cath and this was good news. There was still the tricuspid valve regurgitation and the vasospasm problem in the coronary arteries, but Dr. Crumbley was not yet convinced that the amount of fluid she was accumulating was coming just from her heart. They were pursuing other causes and options.

They still wanted to do that liver cath to check the pressure in the vessels that drain to the liver and a liver biopsy as well. This was scheduled for June 30 at 10:30 AM.. Based on what they might find, they thought they may have a different treatment plan to try to help with some of her fluid retention.

We got the crushing news that Emory would not accept Teresa for transplantation because of her high level of antibodies. Dr. Crumbley said their goal at MUSC was now to keep her as well as they could for as long as they could. To keep that "something to hope for" I would continue to tell our girl, "And who knows what they will know about antibodies and all the rest of this within the upcoming months and years? We know that God will provide an answer in His time."

I never forget Dr. Crumbley looking at Teresa when he gave her the Emory news and saying to her, "You know, all of us here love you with a fervor, and we are going to do the best we can for you."

He also said he could refer her to Duke to see what they would say, but Teresa wanted to give this liver test and subsequent possible treatment he suggested a try. Her thought was that, "I don't think I want to get a risky transplant that might fail in a year if this heart I have will go for a while longer and they may know more and be better able to transplant me somewhere."

She did have that liver cath and biopsy done the following Monday and it went well. It was outpatient and we returned to Lexington to await results. She was fairly lethargic that week before July 4 and her heart raced some during that time. We thought that was perhaps a result of the drugs they gave for the procedure and maybe her regimen of usual meds being somewhat off-schedule.

We made a run to MUSC in the middle of the night on July 4 because she had a fast heart rate of 125-130 bpm for about seven hours. It subsided shortly before we got there. They interrogated her pacemaker and found it to be a run of atrial tachycardia but could not identify a cause. They let her come back home the next morning and told her to go to the ER and have a 12-lead EKG done if it reoccurred. It did not reocccur, at least not for that length of time that had prompted our trip to MUSC. She rallied some after the Fourth and seemed to have a bit more energy.

Teresa continued the drains at Lexington Medical Center each week. The fluid collection (about 2.7 liters for two consecutive weeks) was somewhat less than it had been and we were hoping this was a positive downward trend and not the ascites being evasive in the procedures. Teresa's appointment to learn about the liver tests and check in at the heart clinic was July 15. We would find out the next steps in that appointment. Dr. Crumbley was making a plan.

We were thankful to learn that there was no cirrhosis, no fibrosis in her liver. The portal vessel to the liver seemed to be working. These good results, it had been hoped, would enable a shunt to be placed to drain the ascites without the weekly paracenteses. Dr. Crumbley had found that this was not going to be possible, however, because of the thickness of the fluid she was accumulating. He said they did not make a shunt big enough and efficient enough that would not clog and cause a different set of problems. Upon learning this, he had set about finding another solution. He said he had been thinking, searching, and talking with a lot of people who might give some insight into how, why, and what with the ascites she had. As best as we could understand (and I don't pretend that I was smart enough to understand all of what was put before us that day), the situation was this: Much of the fluid still appeared to be a chylous effusion, which meant a leak somewhere in the lymphatic system. The ingestion of fat aggravated this. Teresa certainly needed fat (and other nutrients), since she was "scary thin" now, and he said it was imperative that they do something. While the paracentesis procedures were necessary to give her relief, they were draining the nutrition right out of her every week.

Based on his findings from the people he consulted, Dr. Crumbley came up with a four-part plan: (1) They would reduce her diet once again to a ceiling of 20-30 grams of fat (the kind we see on the nutrition labels) per day (2) Have her take oral medium-chain triglycerides (another kind of fat that can be absorbed into the blood instead of going through the lymphatic system) three times a day; (3) take a drug that would block fat absorption through the intestinal walls, thereby keeping some of the harmful fat out that way; and (4) take a drug that would help with bile and pancreatic flow.

All of the above except (4) were to begin immediately. The drug for step 4 of the plan would need to be administered in the hospital for about a week because it had some side effects, and with Teresa's history of arrhythmias and vasospasms they wanted to watch her when she began to take this. They scheduled her to be admitted on the same day that she was to have her thyroid gland biopsied - that was already scheduled for outpatient on the 28th of July so they would go ahead and put her in that day to begin that drug therapy.

On Caring Bridge I posted: "Thank you for praying that this plan is God's plan. **I** have been praying that, so I have a measure of peace about what was suggested today."

Chapter 44 A Plan Forward

As I think back on what Ree was facing at this point, I try to see the big picture of what her health was like in that July. Truly we were thankful for the careful, measured care she was getting from so many of her providers in the midst of the ongoing problems. They infused hope into every effort. We were thankful that she did not have lymphoma, cirrhosis of the liver and, as we would soon learn from the thyroid biopsy results, there was no thyroid cancer. We were thankful that the pressures in her heart were not dangerously high according to the heart cath in June. We were thankful that the pacemaker seemed to be working for the heart block after some adjustments they had made. We continued to pray for answers for those awful vasospasms, the excessive pulsing in the vessel in her neck (from the tricuspid valve?), her sometimes racing heart, her erratic kidney function and the accompanying lethargy and nausea, and the ascites with its additional problems of nutrition, appetite and weight loss, mobility loss, shortness of breath, and extremely low blood pressure.

Teresa was admitted on July 28 after the thyroid biopsy. We were visited by a couple of cardiologists in the afternoon but the new drug would not start until after the hepatologists and gastroenterologists weighed in - their input was needed regarding any other possible causes for the ascites and other symptoms. These doctors did come in the next day, asked a lot of questions, went out to examine her records further, then returned with more questions. Early in the evening Teresa's nurse told her they did plan to start the drug Octreotide by injection at 9:00 PM. We prayed and asked our friends to pray that there would be only helpful effects and no adverse ones. She was able to eat without nausea on this day – not a huge amount, but an improvement over previous days.

On July 30 Teresa saw a dietician, some of the liver doctors, and the cardiologists. They all seemed to agree they wanted to fight the ascites by reducing fat in Teresa's diet. This would be accomplished with a rather strict diet (again!) and the fat-blocking drug Xenical. At the same time, she needed to consume at least 1500 calories a day to gain any weight at all, which was critical at this point. She was not a candidate for ANY kind of surgery in the condition she was in, they told her. They also told her a bit more about the drug-by-injection, Octreotide, which was supposed to help with bile and pancreatic flow.

She had started well and the plan was that she would do well enough to continue the regimen they were starting in the hospital at home, but she hardly slept during the night of July 30, and on July 31 she threw everything up late in the morning, could not eat or drink for the rest of the day, and began to have bladder issues. They began to explore the possibility that she might have a UTI and we knew we would not be returning to Lexington until that was resolved. Thankfully everything came together enough for us to roll toward home late in the day of August 1.

It had been an eventful day, August 1. She had a paracentesis at MUSC which was only 1.4 liters, a hopeful sign for diminishing ascites. The doctors told her they had determined what they had needed to know in this hospital admission, that the Octreotide drug did not seem to be causing arrhythmias as is sometimes the case. They had finalized the plan that we had anticipated: continue the low-fat (20-30 grams per day) diet, take the MCT (medium chain triglyceride) oil, take the Xenical to block the fat from digesting, and inject herself three times a day with the Octreotide. It was hoped that this plan would heal the chyle leak and diminish the ascites, thus decreasing the frequency of the paracenteses which were draining the nutrition from her. She was to eat as much protein as possible (55 grams per day) and try to take in those 1500 calories.

We begged our Caring Bridge friends for prayers as Teresa embarked on this plan. The meds schedule would be difficult to maintain. One of her immunosuppressant drugs could not be taken within three hours of the Xenical or it would be diminished in effectiveness, and the MCT oil could not be taken too close to the Xenical because it could be blocked out and it was the kind of fat that she needed. Other meds had to be juggled as well, so she had quite a task set before her. We were reminded once again why we called her our "Warrior Princess," partly because of all of the bruises she carried most of the time from all of her treatment, but also because she remained a fighter.

One of the Charleston doctor's goals was to get Teresa further between the paracenteses, and the following Friday she was able to skip a week for the first time in months. While still retaining some fluid, she felt sure it was somewhat less than it had been. She was still not able to eat very much, so there was no significant weight gain yet, but we reassured ourselves by saying that she had not gotten to this point overnight and it might be a gradual process to get back to where they – and we - wanted her to be. Of course we wanted to fast-track any improvement because she was still so very frail, but we continued to remember: God has a plan and a timetable.

We celebrated Teresa's 39th birthday while she was at home during these two weeks. Bradley had had their deck enclosed and made into a porch that she could sit out on and Bradley's parents gave her some porch furniture that she was so very proud of. I remember she texted me pictures of it - she was sitting in one of the chairs and she was all smiles. We had the usual birthday dinner and cake at our house on the Sunday before her birthday, August 12, and of course we took lots of pictures. She was dreadfully thin but still beaming that day, posing with all of us at the table and individually with Preston and Melinda. We gave her some of her gifts that day and then on her actual birthday I gave her a gift certificate to HandPicked, one of her favorite jewelry stores. I hoped to take her there to spend it sometime in the next several weeks.

Chapter 45 Charleston Adventure and School Prep For Preston

The labs that Teresa had had drawn locally had not thrown up alarms and we were thankful for the almost two weeks she and we had in Lexington to enjoy as much normalcy as possible. She did have an appointment scheduled in Charleston for August 14 so we drove down on the 13th. This was a trip that Preston was able to make with us. Often when she had been hospitalized he was in school. Occasionally he would make a trip with them or us – we took a picture of him sleeping in a hospital chair when we all went down with her the night her heart had raced so. Whenever he would get to visit when she was inpatient and Teresa knew he was coming she would really spruce up – makeup and her best gowns and robes and jewelry. She wanted him to see her in the best possible light. She posted Caring Bridge pictures of him in her arms, both smiling. At least once in those last difficult eight months he begged to stay the night in her room with her.

When she was away she tried to talk to him at night by phone. They had this little ritual that ended their conversations. She would say "Sleep tight. Don't let the bed bugs bite," to which he would reply, "And if they do, pinch 'em black and blue." And then they sometimes added other silly rhymes. Finally she would hear his prayers before she hung up. I would see her close her eyes and then in a few moments she would say, "AMEN!" She sometimes skyped him on her iPad from the hospital too. And while it might have seemed to those observing the poor state of her health that she was not able to do so much for Preston physically, she was still very much in charge and aware of what was going on. She registered him for school from her smartphone. She knew about his schedule, paying fees, making sure he had lunch credit on his account, getting him a yearbook in advance, and who his teacher(s) would be. She wanted so much to be there for him to start school. I recall a prior summer (as school was approaching and she remained hospitalized) when she kept telling Bradley and us, "Tell Preston I WILL be back for him to start school." Until this summer, she had been able to do just that.

Between that last hospital stay and this outpatient (we thought it would be) MUSC appointment on August 14, while we were still in Lexington, Teresa, Preston, and I had gone to Deerfield Elementary to register him for the 2014-15 school year. It was a brand new school and we were excited for him. We pushed our sick mom/daughter in and went to the various stations to do what we needed to do. I recall going into the new computer lab where there were stations set up for filling out paperwork, signing documents, reading policies. I don't know why I remember so clearly this one scene, but I recall Teresa reading quietly out loud to Preston every line of the computer/iPad policy. He was not too interested but she wanted to be sure he knew the rules. They were to use the iPads at school for the first time this year. I also recall slipping away from them to speak to the volunteer at a nearby desk who was in charge of school calendars, having to say, "My grandson's mother is VERY sick. May I have an extra school calendar to keep with me?" I cry as I think of that day. Everyone at Deerfield Elementary would turn out to be wonderful for Preston and again I give thanks for every one of them. He had, in fact, had wonderful teachers from preschool forward, and I never forget Lexington Baptist Preschool or Pleasant Hill Elementary and the wonderful staffs there either.

I think Teresa may have had a feeling that she might not be in Lexington for the start of school in 2014, because she wanted to take Preston on that August 13 afternoon to the Charleston mall where we sometimes shopped and find some clothes for him. Preston and I took turns pushing Teresa in her chair and she and he found him some things to wear to school. It was amazing to me how quickly she knew just what he would like and **not** like and exactly what size to get to allow for comfort, style and growth. Some of those shirts and other clothes she bought that day he wore all through fourth grade and even into the next year too. It was another happy keeper memory for the three of us from that afternoon and Teresa was proud to have been able to accomplish what she did.

That scheduled appointment the next morning, August 14, brought mixed news. The doctor was happy that she was able to skip a week of having the paracentesis procedures and glad that the new drugs seemed to be helping the fluid; however, her creatinine was significantly elevated, indicating kidney troubles again, so much so that they admitted her to the hospital to try to find out why. So she and her Preston had to part –he and I drove home on Thursday evening and Bradley drove to Charleston to be with Teresa over the weekend. Terry and I would go with Preston to Open House at Deerfield Elementary on Sunday afternoon, then take him to Nana and return to MUSC, where I would stay with Teresa in the hospital while Bradley and Terry returned to Lexington to work.

Teresa was very concerned about Preston's school year. She texted me by phone before the Open House: "Meet the teacher, Mama. PLEASE let me know how she is. He does not need a sick mom AND a mean teacher." I cry as I write that line too and once again give thanks for Mrs. Harte, who was experienced in another state but new to Deerfield. She was wonderful to Preston as the year began and I think her name should have been spelled "Heart" instead of "Harte." When she had to leave her position to care for an ill family member, Mrs. Simon stepped into fourth grade and she also helped to meet a big need for our boy that year.

As I left the Open House that August afternoon I was able to reassure Teresa by phone that Preston would be well taken care of for school in the upcoming year. I knew her heart was breaking that she was not there for this important day.

Chapter 46 Life is Hard But God is Good

August 14 – 21 rolled by and on August 22 Teresa was still inpatient. She had struggled so with the poor kidney function, no appetite or energy, further weight loss, nausea, horrid diarrhea, low low blood pressure, accumulating ascites, juggling of medicines, etc. A host of doctors weighed in on her case, trying to get the pieces of the puzzle to fit. They were gallantly trying and she was valiantly fighting. They had even tested for C-Diff, that awful potentially life-threatening bacteria that affects the colon. Thankfully she did not test positive for that, and by the 22nd her kidneys were finally beginning to improve and she could eat a bit better and keep it. All of this seemed like gradual progress, certainly from the standpoint of her status upon admission.

They were beginning to talk about a feeding tube for nutrition but were doing all they could to avoid that. They continued to diurese her in IV and wanted to transition her to oral diuretics as soon as they could and if it worked they hoped to get her home again. Once again, Bradley and I were tag-teaming. He would get to MUSC as soon as he could for the weekend and I would return to Lexington. She had never spent a night in the hospital by herself and we never meant for her to if we could help it. She always looked so forward to Bradley walking through that hospital room door.

Remember the Christian song from years ago, "Life is Hard but God is Good?" This was so true for this hospital stay, as it had been for many others. We continued to thank on Caring Bridge everyone who had been on their knees for us.

On August 25 they were able to discharge Teresa and we reached her house about 5:30 PM. She arrived with lots of nutritional supplements, the injectable Octreotide (which Dr. Crumbley had gone to battle with the insurance company to pay and he won!), some change in diuretics, and the usual regimen of other meds. She was eating somewhat better and while she was still retaining fluid, that seemed some better too.

Upon discharge they still were considering the serious solutions of feeding tube and/or dialysis. They had held off on these when her creatinine came down – not to normal but much better than it had been. They wanted to keep close watch through lab work and told her they wanted to see her back there about once a week for a while. They would call us for the next appointment.

Teresa was somewhat limited in activity, but she wanted to do as much as she could. I wrote on Caring Bridge on August 26, "Want you to know that Teresa is not bedbound now that she is home. She can sit, walk short distances, watch TV, read, talk with family, make plans (for herself and all of us!), keep up with her medicine, use her phone and computer, etc. Terry and/or I (and Bradley and Preston, of course) can still take her places when she feels like going. Certainly we know how and why all of this is possible - the prayers of the faithful."

We don't believe the prayers ever stopped.

Chapter 47 September 2, 2014

The following weekend was Labor Day. Preston was asked to go to the beach with a friend's family. Teresa loved Ryan and knew what a good time Preston would have with him and she wanted him to be out there having fun when he could. So we got his bags packed at her direction and he went off and did, indeed, have a wonderful time. He got back on Monday in time to prepare for school the next day and, as I remember Bradley saying later, get covered with his Mama's hugs and kisses before bedtime.

Teresa called me early on the morning of September 2. Bradley was getting ready to take Preston to school and then go on to work. She had had vasospasms in the night (as she had continued to do off and on along with her other health issues) and wanted me to come and be with her sooner than usual. She was going to try to go back to sleep, but I prepared to go right away. Bradley would be starting toward school and work while I was traveling the fourteen miles to their house.

When I got there she was indeed sleeping like a baby. The bed Bradley had gotten her was an adjustable one and she was able to breathe better if she could just recline instead of lie flat. She was so very thin and this mattress was plush and easy on her skin. She looked peaceful there and I spoke softly to her. She said she was okay at the moment and just wanted to sleep. I watched and waited for a while, then decided, since I felt assured that she was content and comfortable, that I would zip around to the McDonald's not so far down the way and get a cup of coffee. That done, I settled in again. As the time wore on I began to fret about her taking the medicine she was supposed to take at a certain time.

I went into her bedroom and called her name. Her eyelids fluttered open. I asked if I could bring her medicine in but she said, "No, I'm going to get up in a little bit and come out there." In maybe fifteen minutes I went to inquire again. Again she said she was going to get up. And sure enough she did rouse up before long and make her way to her recliner. She seemed weak and exhausted, though, and I did not want to question her too much about the vasospasms. I did ask her about her medicines and she said, "In a little while."

Then she said something that alarmed me. She said, "Mama, there is stuff all over my back. Get something and wash it off, please." I got a clean warm washcloth and went to her and sponged her back. While I had been concerned about what was there, I became even more alarmed when I discovered that there was **nothing** there. I didn't know what had caused her to think there was. I simply asked, "Is that better?" to which she responded, "Yes, much better. Thanks."

As I walked into her kitchen after this task I remember thinking, "I am going to have to get her to MUSC this day. Will I be able to take her myself in my car or do I need to call an ambulance?"

She asked me for her medicine. I knew she needed her immunosuppressants and the injection of Octreotide right away. She was able to tell me exactly which medicines and how much of each, so that reassured me somewhat. I went back to her den and set them on the table beside her chair. There were so many things to take and she never liked to be stood over until she had taken them all, even in the hospital when the nurses would bring them in. While she could swallow a handful of pills at a time, she knew herself and knew when she had the stomach to do it. I moved from her chair just a few feet to the couch and began to fold the clean laundry that was there. I was standing facing her. She had begun to gradually take the medicine. I saw her shoot her nitro spray, which signaled to me that she was having another vasospasm. In just a moment Teresa made a move as if to get up from her chair, pushing up on the arms of the recliner. I thought perhaps she was rising to go back to the bathroom. When she leaned forward she fell face-up to the carpeted floor in front of her recliner. I was but a few steps away and when I got to her and dropped to my knees I knew she was close to heaven if not already there.

I called 911 from my cell phone and the dispatcher was professional and competent. The ambulance got there quickly. My hands were still on my girl, believing in my heart that she was gone from us now but allowing them to do what they deemed necessary. They asked me if she had a Do Not Resuscitate directive and I told them she did not. They began their work. While I remember being beside myself I also remember feeling, deep down below the hysteria, a calm assurance that God had her now and this was how He had decided to heal her. **My** heart would always and completely be broken for the loss of her, but hers was now forever well, no more struggling to walk and eat and even breathe, no more hateful vasospasms. I managed to call Terry and Bradley and they came quickly and got there before they loaded our Ree into that ambulance. Terry says he remembers coming through that door and knowing, feeling she was not there. I asked the paramedics, "She's gone, isn't she?" to which they responded, "We are doing everything we can, Ma'am." While we had to have known in our deepest denying parts, Bradley, Terry, and me, that she was gradually leaving us throughout these long hard months, we were numb and stunned as we stood in Teresa's kitchen in those early moments.

We followed the ambulance, managing to call Melinda and our friend Penny, who met us at the hospital along with Homer and Betty and J.K. Nella, Bradley's mom, came to be with us too. We were not there long before the doctor came out with the news we already knew. Teresa's hard fight was over. They asked us if we wanted to see her once more. I did. When we got to her room she looked as though she had fallen asleep – peaceful, no sign of pain or worry or struggle on her sweet face. Even while I felt that chasm of darkness that would always be our earthly longing for her encompass me, I could feel too that sweet relief for her that meant her release from all that had tormented her here. She had surely wanted to stay, no doubt. She was surely in that better place, also beyond doubt. I hold that belief in my heart every day.

I had to call my sweet sister and tell her by phone. Even though she did not use social media I was afraid that she might get word somehow before I could physically get there. Fay was distraught and disbelieving but she got herself together for me in that moment and assured us that she and Chalmers would pray and make plans to see us.

Bradley wanted us to go with him to tell Preston. He asked us not to cry. Preston's Granddaddy Taylor had gone to school to get him and he brought him back to the car lot. We all gathered together in a back room and Bradley told him that Jesus had come to "scoop Mama up in His arms" to take her to heaven where she would not be sick any more. Preston cried, of course, but while he was stunned and shocked and sad, I think he knew, even as Teresa had tried to "bear up" through all of her recent suffering, how very, very sick his mom had been. In the days ahead he would miss her terribly and more than once he would say, and sometimes scream, heart-wrenchingly, "If MY MOM was here...if she was just here..."

Terry and I went back to our house late that afternoon and fell into the arms of our church friends who were there waiting. Neighbors and other friends came to comfort. I never forget Larry, our neighbor across the street, walking over and grabbing me in a hug in our driveway. He said, "Miz Ruthie, I wanted to be sure you saw the rainbow that's in the sky this afternoon," and he pointed to it. I never see a rainbow since that day that I don't think of Teresa being in heaven and how God reminded me through my neighbor to "look up."

I wrote on Caring Bridge to our many friends and soldiers, "Today God healed our Warrior Princess. Teresa is with Jesus. Our hearts are broken and will forever be altered, but we are joyful for her release from suffering. We know where she is. She did indeed fight the good fight. Certainly we need your prayers each time you think of us - keep us as close to the Father as you can."

Chapter 48 A Warrior's Funeral

What were those early hours and days of loss like? How did we get through them? What occupied our minds, filled our hearts, fueled our thoughts, drove our actions? How did we survive? Did we do well? Did we blame someone? Did we make promises to ourselves, to Teresa, to others, and if so, did we keep those promises? Were we overwhelmed with sorrow or anger or regrets? Did the darkness come for us? Even now I cannot answer completely or accurately all of these questions.

Most immediately we had to plan a funeral for a warrior. When we asked Bradley where he wanted to bury Teresa he could only answer, "Somewhere pretty." So we chose a hillside in a local cemetery that overlooks a pond. It is not so far from the house where she grew up, where she went to school and to church, where she played with young friends and made older ones. We made plans to bury the rest of us beside her.

I hardly knew how to write Teresa's obituary. Always later I think of something I omitted or said not just right, but what I wrote was:

> *Today our sweet Teresa dances and sings with the angels. She lived her life much loved, suffered with dignity, and left behind a myriad of life lessons.*
>
> *Teresa was born on August 12, 1975 and lived her entire life in Lexington County. She was educated in Lexington County District One public schools and at Midlands Technical College. She worked for Jim Sketo and Rick Hall in Lexington as a legal assistant her entire adult work career.*
>
> *Teresa married her childhood sweetheart Bradley Taylor in 1998 and in 2004 Preston Henry Taylor came into their family. It was for her "two boys" that Teresa struggled and fought so hard to stay here. Not knowing everything about our heavenly home except that it will be magnificent, we speculate that, insofar as the Heavenly Father allows, she still watches over them.*
>
> *Teresa also steadfastly loved, and was steadfastly loved by, her Daddy and Ma, Terry and Cornelia Ruth Edwards of*

Lexington, her sister Melinda Edwards of Columbia, her Aunt Fay (Uncle Chalmers) Hancock of Saluda, and all of her Power and Edwards uncles, aunts, and cousins as well as her parents-in-law Drayton and Nella Taylor of Lexington, brothers-in-law Martin Taylor and Kevin Taylor (Selena) and her niece Sederis.

She is welcomed into eternal rest by her grandparents Henry and Margaret Power and Joe and Clara Edwards along with other special family members and, we suspect, a Chihuahua named Zack.

For the gift of organ donation we can never pray enough thanks. The transplanted heart that extended and enriched Teresa's life for fourteen years was a gift beyond expression. To the staff at MUSC who infused hope into their every effort and to the Radiology staff at Lexington Medical Center who made her last days more comfortable with the weekly procedures done there, we appreciate you from the deepest parts of our souls.

When Teresa was five years old, she came to faith and never wavered from it. Her earthly church membership was at Oakwood Baptist Church. As she enters that eternal palace, we feel that she will be able to say to the Great Comforter, "I have fought the good fight, I have finished the race, I have kept the faith." 2 Timothy 4: 7 (NIV)

On September 5, a Friday morning, we made our way to our beloved Oakwood Baptist Church. I can see the faces of Janet and William Hentz as they ministered to our family on behalf of the food services committee with a refreshment table near the choir room. I can see the men of our church scurrying about bringing in extra chairs and making sure all was in order. In that choir room our family had gathered and our pastor came and prayed with us before the service began. I felt a strange peace as we lined up and filed into the church at 11:00 that day. I had asked for the song, "When We All Get to Heaven" and the music filled our sanctuary.

We had met with Pastor Rich earlier in the week about Teresa's eulogy. Rich had married Teresa and Bradley, dedicated their child, and supported them throughout the transplant. I had written some words for her eulogy which he presented in her service as a message from her family:

Teresa was named for her Daddy and for her Aunt Fay, her mama's sister. Teresa was her Grandma Tulie's sweetness and Grandma Clara's stoicism all rolled together. This was no crybaby!

We knew from the beginning of her diagnosis 27 years ago that she probably would not make it into our old age with us. We think she realized this not so long after, so she got busy living. To say this was an easy path would be an untruth. But to say we have not been immeasurably blessed would be more of an untruth:

We saw repeated miracles of healing. We learned lessons in depending only on God and the power and strength He sent so many, many times. We came to a recognition of the specialized gifts God has given his various servants and the countless ways love can be expressed.

*You may have heard us call her our "Warrior Princess" and that is what she was. She fought hard to stay with us for as long as she could. Once a nurse commented in the hospital that she looked not sick, but well, to which Teresa responded, "I want to **feel** well and **be** well, so I try to **look** well." Every morning of every hospital stay, she would instruct whichever of us was with her, "Bring me that pink bag," and out would come the makeup, hairbrush, toothbrush, and all of the other things she needed to "get her look on."*

*She realized that looks were not the most important thing, though, and she kept her faith intact. She shared that faith with her boy even when she was away from him. Almost every night at the hospital she could be heard on the phone, saying, "Ok, I'm ready. And after a few minutes we would hear, "**Aaa**men."*

We believe Teresa is thanking the Father for so many things today, as we are:

***Thankful** that she had as normal a childhood as any kid, swimming, skating, riding horses, dancing, taking gymnastics, riding a bicycle, playing piano, romping with her family.*

Thankful *that she knew all of her grandparents before they went to heaven. Thankful for a baby sister, whose picture she showed off whenever she got the chance. Thankful for **all** of the Edwardses and Powers and Taylors and Millers who loved her until the end.*

Thankful *that she met the man of her dreams in the heart of a thirteen-year-old boy and never turned him loose, and vice versa!*

Thankful *for the little man that completed her family in 2004, a boy who amazed her on every hand and whose future she has surely molded.*

Thankful *for her many friends from childhood forward who were her cheerleaders in every game.*

(Portion of an email we had received from a friend, which Rich included in the eulogy):

> *No words from me tonight, except..... Thank you God in heaven for Teresa's life, for her inspiration to me and my family, for the times I was blessed enough to share with her, before, during and after her heart transplant... for the bond that she and I were able to make, for the love that poured from her very soul for her mother, father, sister, husband and precious son Preston. For the purpose of her life here.... to be an unwavering example of faith, courage and dedication to you. Oh Lord....... her fight to stay alive is over...... the battle is won........ Thank you, God in heaven, for sharing your child with us. She was your light here, and now is at home with you.*

Thankful *for a work career among Christian people for as long as she could work.*

(Portion of email from Jim Sketo, her boss):

> *...You know how very much we all loved Teresa. She was kind and very smart. She has been away from the office a while now and we still call her desk & computer "Teresa's ".....That won't change. She and I did over 15,000 Right of Way Opinions together. She knew when my blood sugars were high, when my vision was blurred or even when I had angina by looking at my work. And she never asked (about my documents), "What does this say?" .....She*

was exceptional!!!!! But you and your family know how very special she was. We grew to love you all as family....

Thankful *for a donated heart from a grieving family whose loved one spoke life to our family for fourteen years beyond what we might otherwise have had.*

Thankful *that she never had to spend a night in a hospital – ever – without a family member there.*

Thankful *for every person connected to the medical world who connected with her world. The dedication and the effort and the hope and the love have been unbelievable. Thankful that for every time they had to scratch their heads and collaborate for a solution, they always came up with a plan that gave her hope, a hope that indeed lasted until that last breath.*

(The following are emails, or portions thereof, from medical staff at MUSC.)

From the transplant surgeon:

Kathy Law called me with the news a little while ago. I was so hopeful that we were getting ahead of the ascites. Who would have thought it would be the vasospasm? Unfortunately, we just never know what God's plan is for us. All we are allowed to do is to try to do the right thing. Please note that my thoughts and prayers are with you all during this time of terrible sadness. I was so fond of her and constantly amazed by her perpetual strength and beauty, inside and out. I know that offering seems hollow at this point, but you know you can count on me and any of us to do whatever we can for you and your family. You will always be a part of the MUSC Transplant Team.

From one of the transplant team nurses:

I am so very saddened to hear of Teresa's passing. I can't stop thinking about you and your family. We are all just so heartbroken for you all. She was one of my favorite patients and I always looked forward to seeing you both. Her strength and kind nature will forever inspire me in my own life to be a better mother and friend. She never complained or succumbed to self-pity. She radiated positivity. She endured so much at such a young age, and handled it with such grace. I know that she has finally found peace and comfort.

I keep thinking about our talk last week in the hospital, when she shared the story about her son. I could tell how much she loved him. I felt honored that she shared that with me. I felt honored to be a part of the team who had the opportunity to care for her.

I drove over the James Island connector last night thinking about you and Teresa, and there was the most beautiful sunset. It began to rain lightly, which produced a rainbow. It made me smile, and I felt it was a sign that Teresa was smiling down from heaven.

*And most of all, **thankful** that after her last breath, she realized the fulfilment of that greatest of all hopes, which she owned since age five when she accepted Jesus and sealed her place in heaven. We are certain of where she is today.*

Along with our words of remembrance Rich also delivered a wonderful message relating Teresa's physical heart transplant and healing to our spiritual heart's transformation and growth when we accept our Saviour. He made us aware of the complete circle of our lives that God orchestrates and reminded us that He always knows and plans the best for us. Our friend and former pastor Steve Eargle gave the closing prayer. Our church was filled up that day with family and friends and in the days that followed the support and encouragement flowed out of these and many others to pave our way forward. I told some who came through a very long line to speak to us that our plans were to "Put one foot in front of the other, just as Teresa did, **every** day that she lived."

Chapter 49 Stumbling Ahead

There were gaping holes in all of us. Terry and I worried for Bradley – he was broken into a thousand pieces. He had friends and family who rallied around him and Preston, but his heart was so thoroughly shattered. We fretted for Preston, who missed his mom at such a vulnerable age and at the start of a new school year. His jagged little heart reached for her touch and her love and her care for him. His teachers, friends, and family stepped up to do what they could for him. A number of staff from throughout the school district had been present at Teresa's funeral. Many were my former colleagues and friends and a number of them were Preston's teachers, present and former, and most of these had known Teresa throughout the years.

Besides those already named in Teresa's story, the faces of other friends flash across my memory, too many to include but always with me. Mary Pearce, whom Teresa had encouraged toward transplant and who was still doing so well these thirteen years later, came to Teresa's funeral. Those who had experienced loss stepped up: Vanna's parents and brother were at the funeral and Louise Parker, who had lost a daughter in childhood, reached out to us. Beth Pepin, with whom I had worked earlier in my career in Lexington District One, persisted in prayer and checking on me. These are representative of the amazing outpouring of God's love.

My friend Karen Rudd asked me for some of Teresa's clothes, particularly some that she had worn recently. I gathered them and took to her at church and what she did was an amazing act of love that did more for Preston than I can ever describe in words. Karen's friend had received the talent of making stuffed animals for children out of the clothing of their loved one. I had sent several articles of clothing, a couple of which Teresa had worn quite often because they were so comfortable there at the end. Karen had two animals made. I let Preston choose which one to keep at his house. He did not hesitate at instantly picking the one dressed in the shirt and pants his mom had worn most frequently. He said, "I pick Mama." That's how real this bear was to him and it got him through many a sad night. I never ever forget this kindness.

Teresa's friend Gayle had asked Terry for some of the flowers from Teresa's casket spray. He willingly gave them. Several weeks later Gayle showed up with necklaces she had had a jewelry designer make from the flowers. She had one made for Melinda, one for me, and one for her - another treasured kindness that stays with me always. It keeps Teresa close and remembrance of the friends she had here close as well.

There is another jewelry story to tell. The first time I went out into the world to do something that felt "normal" a few weeks after Teresa died, I went to a local department store and began to just walk around the store. Not really having a need but needing to stay busy and moving, I had chosen this particular activity to pass the time. I never bought expensive rings or necklaces for myself, but I loved looking at the little silver "knuckle" rings in the jewelry section that Teresa had actually started me to wearing years before. This one little inexpensive ring spoke to me that day. It had a simple design but not totally plain – there was a kind of scroll or loop in the metal that got my attention. I found one that seemed to fit and purchased it. When I got in my car and put the ring on, I noticed that it was not a simple loop or scroll at all but a treble clef! Now I don't consider myself a musician by any stretch, my only talent being some very basic piano skills, so I would not have bought this as an expression of my talent or personality, but for some reason I decided to keep it. I turned the radio on as I pulled out of the parking lot that day and "Blessings' by Laura Story began to play. I felt with all my heart that God let Teresa speak to me that afternoon.

A stoic sort of depression, for lack of a better description, settled on Terry. It frightened me. It was like a cloak, this sadness that we wore. One thing Terry knew he could do was keep Teresa's grave in order. He went there daily at first and for a long time after. He sprigged and he fertilized and he kept the ants off. He watered. He cried. His heart spilled out at that gravesite and he continues to manage that, often saying, "Daddy's got this, Ree." He carefully considers her flowers and he cleans the marker. She would be proud. On birthdays we have taken Preston there and tied some birthday balloons onto the grave flowers and released some into the sky. While I believe Teresa sees things differently from there in heaven – more about that in a moment – I also believe that the one thing she would want most from us here is not to be forgotten. We talk of her often to Preston about how much she loved him and his dad. We remind him with words as well as pictures of the things she enjoyed, what she treasured, the work she did, the fun she had, her hopes for his life. It is comforting to speak of her and have others recall her with joy.

The tributes to Teresa that found their way to us and the Taylors during those early months were astounding, strengthening, and numerous. As in the days of Teresa's hospitalization they came in many forms – visits, cards, emails, phone calls, Caring Bridge, the online computer guest books where her obituary had appeared, donations in her memory. I wanted to respond to each one but knew I never could adequately say thank you. I tried. As I think even now of those countless messages I see the faces and names of their senders in the shape of angels in my mind and heart. I wish I could gather them all into one of those word clouds and make a literal rendering of that angel to set in the midst of all of our world's troubled ones.

Aunt Fay wrote a letter to Teresa, beautifully recalling memories from her childhood forward that engrave her so indelibly in our family history: picking flowers outside, piano and dance recitals, gymnastic performances, the time she and Bradley dressed as Raggedy Ann and Andy and drove to Saluda to show her, all those Christmases she had lived and loved. Fay even remembered those midnight French fries! Her letter includes, "We all know you lived a life here of love and grace. Your beautiful smile and lilting voice will always be with me...I pray God will continue to let me feel you close to me."

Chapter 50 Heaven...

Teresa's friend Sundai Hall wrote a beautiful tribute to her that she gave to me just shortly after the funeral. In it Sundai writes from Teresa's point of view as she entered heaven. It is beautiful to me and I begged her to publish it somewhere. What she said to me was, "No, Mrs. Ruth, you can just include it in your book if you want to." I **do** want to:

Teresa and God's conversation on entering Heaven (from Sundai's perspective...):

Teresa: *Lord, I love you and I am so happy to be here, but was this what was really supposed to happen to me? I mean, all the struggle to live to see the next day, the days in the hospital, the reliance on my parents for my very day-to-day needs to be met, even though I'm married and have a son – why did this happen when I could have done so much more for all of them had I been healthy enough to live and prosper? Is this really what your plan was?* (Questions we all would like to know the answers to as well... and Teresa surely has asked!)

The Lord: *Yes, this was the plan... And you did very well, my child. You honored me in the good... and in your struggles, which were many. And you did better than I expected you would, because:*

You accepted me and gave me the glory in your childhood, even though you didn't know why your energy level was weak.

You gave me the glory when you got through school and got your first job.

You gave me praise and thanks when your middle school boyfriend asked you to marry him.

You trusted me when you knew your heart was weak and failing.

You gave me the glory for your heart transplant.

You gave me the glory for your recovery from the transplant surgery, even though you struggled with so many issues through all of it.

And Teresa, people watched as you gave me the glory for your recovery.

People watched as you were so bold and courageous to adopt my child Preston who needed loving parents and a stable Christian home.

People watched as you lived courageously, working so that you could relieve some financial burden from your husband and your mom and dad.

People watched as you gently and respectfully glided through the following years as a loving mother, wife, daughter, and friend, although some days you were depressed because you had to continue to take all of the meds and live such a strict life under the microscope of constant doctors' appointments... all the while praising my name and being overwhelmed by my grace which carried you on a daily basis.

Teresa: *But Lord, the last few years, when things started going wrong and I was trying so hard to stay alive and my mother stayed by my side to be sure my commitment to life was strong, did you know then that you would bring me home to heaven instead of letting me see* ***my*** *goal in life: To be successful in living and watch my son grow up and graduate from high school, grow old with Bradley, and see Preston get married and, you know, be a grandmother?*

Did, you, Lord, did you let me try so hard every day and have hope in my heart that you were going to pull me through this? Did you let my mom try so hard to love me through only to realize that my goal was going to be a failure?

God: *Yes, my precious Teresa, I did. You see, through all of these years your faith was enhanced, your relationship with me was made rock solid, as well as your mother's relationship with me, and both of you bonded in a way that proved to others that endurance and faith and trust in me is the pinnacle of being my worthy servant and child.*

I protected you from an earlier death. People had time to see what you did with the miracle of the heart transplant.

People had time to see you prosper from the miracle, and people had time to say goodbye. And people had time to watch your reaction and your mother's reaction to everything you were going through on a weekly or monthly basis.

I saw all of this. I was with you and your mom every minute. People saw the demonstration of what my GRACE truly is, what LOVE truly is, what FAITH truly is. People you knew were inspired by you and by your family.

People saw the resilience in your son Preston and his innocence in knowing that Mama can eat donuts every day if she wants... so long as it makes her gain some weight. They saw the pictures of Preston sleeping in the hospital chair next to your bed while visiting with you. They saw the love of a son for his mother tested at such an early age. They saw his smile every time he saw YOU because he knew his world would be complete as long as you were there and in it. And your world was complete too. You gave me the honor and praise on your Christmas card when you wrote about how grateful you were for your life, your family, and that this was "My world."

People saw your parents and Bradley's come together to support you and Preston and saw the loyalty in family that was necessary to get through a life-changing battle such as yours was. May I say that most families would have failed this test?

People saw time ticking away and chose to believe the end for you was further away than it really was. I saw the priorities in those who came and comforted and stayed connected to you and to your cause, which was to stay alive, no matter how much it hurt... Those who thought there was more time are now sad and disappointed that their best efforts at seeing you before the end were shattered because they weren't in control of seeing the beginning or the end, only I was. Those people are reminded that I, Your God, am the only one that knows the true date and time of one's entrance onto earth and departure from earth.

Many people witnessed your commitment to me, including your doctors and dear nurses, and let's not forget those patients that were there with you through the years, those whom you also influenced by your faith and your trust in the future, and in me. How do you think they would have made it without your example? You fulfilled your witnessing for me and I am proud of that.

Teresa: *Yes, Lord, I know that others were along on the ride with me through all of this, but I never thought of it the way you are explaining it to me now. I only had* ***my*** *goal in mind: to live, to be a wife, mother, daughter, sister and friend for a little longer. I was fearful of you taking me too soon and that's why I fought so hard to stay.*

Lord, I didn't want to leave when you called me on Tuesday, but I didn't want to risk not being called by you again, so I came home, trusting YOU. As I had trusted you all the years before, I trusted you on Tuesday morning that You would watch over and take care of my precious Preston and Bradley, that you would comfort my mom, dad and sister, my other family members, and all those friends who are now grieving for me, and who are most likely at my church right now to comfort my family at my funeral. Lord, I want you to give them a sign that I'm okay and I made it home with you. In your own way and time, please send them that sign.

I trusted you on Tuesday when I told myself, 'It's time to let happen what ***HE*** *wants to happen, not what* ***I*** *want to happen, even though it was a bittersweet parting with my life on earth. I realize now that Heaven is safe, beautiful, secure, and that I can lay down ALL of my struggles, and Lord, that is a BIG relief to me. So I thank you, Lord.*

God: *Teresa, I love you so much. I created the fiber of your being before you were born, and I gave you to Ruth and Terry knowing that they would be strong enough to travel through your life with you. I placed Bradley in your life because he is strong enough, too, and I knew you would inspire him and that he would be a better man for your being his wife. I gave both of you Preston because Preston deserved loving and devoted and Christian parents. I never once had doubts that you were not strong enough or determined enough or dedicated to me enough to pass the life test that you have been taking for 39 years.*

My dear child, no more pain, no more hospitals, no more tests and doctors and nurses and worrying for those around you that you love so much. No more scars, procedures, wonder of why this is happening, no more dark nights, no more tears, no more anxiety over Bradley or Preston or your parents because of your illness. Teresa, IT IS FINISHED, it is done, and you have ACED your life test.

You, my child, have exceeded the challenges I set before you and you have earned your place in my Kingdom of Heaven and I am happy you answered me on Tuesday morning when I reached out for you to call you home.

(Teresa smiles and gives a nod of her head to her Lord, and a tear of joy streams down her face. Jesus takes her in his arms and hugs her with a hug that only the One that loves us the most would give.)

Now go and enjoy the fruits of the Kingdom, reunite with your loved ones who are here, continue to praise my name and continue to be a blessing to others by your infinite knowledge of what an angel does on earth and what an angel does in heaven, as both have ministered to you in the journey. You will do your job very well here too, my sweet and faithful servant, although it will be much easier and much more fulfilling than the job I gave you on earth.

Do not worry about your loved ones. They will miss you indeed, but the strength and courage and the faith you showed them you had in Me has truly been digested by them. They will one day enter into this Kingdom and live and forever be reunited with you.

Teresa: (Deep breath) *Okay, Lord, thank you, thank you,* (falling to her knees) *and thank you again.*

God: *Do you have any more questions?*

Teresa: *Yes, Lord, one more.... Is my dog Zack up here too?*

God: (A laugh erupts from the Almighty) *Go, now, my child, and reap your blessings and rewards I have in store for you...*

What comfort Sundai brought to me in this tribute and while I know that I fall far short of her descriptions here, I do **want** to be that stalwart, faithful, persevering person. "I press on toward the goal to win the prize for which God has called me ...." Philippians 3:14 (NIV) What I do know is that my warrior fought with all she had and God sent an army of soldiers and angels to help her do that. I feel privileged to have been in the ranks.

What I also continue to know is that Teresa is happy there in heaven and she now sees things so much differently. I believe that about heaven. While we never forget the personality, character, and outlook on life that Teresa Fay Edwards Taylor had here, there, THERE in all of the beauty of heaven, she has a brilliant, glorious clarity, a beauty and a peace and a fulfillment that are something we can't understand this side of it. But I already embrace it and look forward to it. I expect to see her there.

Today as I sit at my computer I still grieve. I will always grieve, this I know. I loved my girl her whole life and took the best care I could of her for twenty-seven years after her diagnosis. Today even more than earlier I think of the woman she would have been today if she had not been sick, and I miss that woman. I tell the Lord I hope that is not a sin. "Father, you gave me two beautiful daughters. I thank you for the one in Asheville and the one in heaven. Forgive me if I wish Teresa could see how her boy has grown and the joy he continues to grow in us. Forgive me if I wish she had been here to see Melinda fall in love with Matt and get married on that mountainside in Asheville and then bring baby May into our lives. I know she was a beach girl but wouldn't she be happy for our mountain shack? Maybe that's You, Lord, letting her speak your love and hers to us in the fireflies, songbirds, wild turkeys, and the water rushing below us in the creek. Have you sent those hummingbirds to Bradley and Preston's kitchen window every single summer since she left here? I don't know how it all works there, but if You wouldn't mind arranging it, please let her know we will always love her. And we'll be seeing her in what, for all of you there, I feel sure, is just a moment."

I feel Teresa advising us from that safe, healthy, happy eternity, "Don't stumble in the shadow of my death, but dance in the light that my life shone into yours." I may not be even as good a dancer as I am a card player, but I try to remind my heart to dance, every day ... in the light God shines on me through a Warrior Princess.

"My grace is sufficient for you..." II Corinthians 12:9a (NKJV)

Made in the USA
Columbia, SC
27 May 2019